Salvador da Bahia, Brazil

Sandra Wilkins

Contents

Articles

Overview of Bahia   **1**
- Bahia   1
- Samba   17
- Capoeira   32

Overview of Salvador   **44**
- Salvador, Bahia   44

Cityscape   **74**
- Barra (neighborhood)   74
- Brotas (neighbourhood)   78
- Cajazeiras (neighbourhood)   79
- Caminho das Árvores (neighbourhood)   79
- Campo Grande (neighbourhood)   79
- Graça (neighborhood)   79
- Historic Centre (Salvador, Bahia)   80
- Itaigara (neighbourhood)   84
- Itapoã (neighbourhood)   84
- Liberdade (neighbourhood)   85
- Ondina (neighbourhood)   86
- Pituba (neighbourhood)   87
- Rio Vermelho (neighbourhood)   89
- Vitória (neighbourhood)   89
- Periperi   91

Attractions in and Around the City   **93**

Museu Rodin Bahia	93
Cathedral of Salvador	93
São Francisco Church and Convent	95
Church of Nosso Senhor do Bonfim, Salvador	97
September Seven Avenue	100
Oceanic Avenue	101
Bahian Carnival	102
Grande Sertão Veredas National Park	104
Abrolhos Marine National Park	105
Chapada Diamantina National Park	106
Morro de São Paulo	108
Itaparica Island	112
Sincura	112
Porto da Barra Beach	113
Baía de Todos os Santos	114
Esporte Clube Bahia	115
Galícia Esporte Clube	122
Associação Desportiva Leônico	125
Esporte Clube Vitória	126
Esporte Clube Ypiranga	132
ATP Itaparica	134
Estádio Parque Santiago	135
Estádio de Pituaçu	136
Estádio Fonte Nova	137
Barradão	140

Cities Nearby with Attractions　　142

Porto Seguro	142
Feira de Santana	147
Vitória da Conquista	149

Ilhéus	151
Itabuna	157
Jequié	158
Lauro de Freitas	159
Cachoeira	159
Juazeiro	161

Transportation — 163

Deputado Luís Eduardo Magalhães International Airport	163
Salvador Metro	168
Port of Salvador	170

References

Article Sources and Contributors	172
Image Sources, Licenses and Contributors	174

Overview of Bahia

Bahia

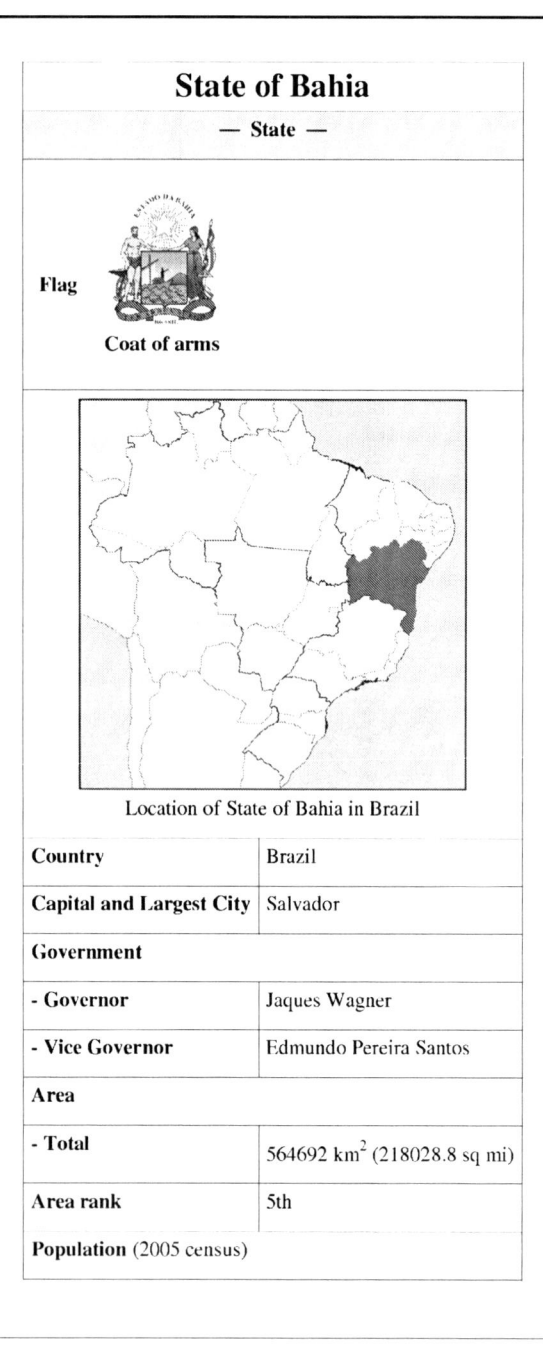

State of Bahia	
— State —	
Flag Coat of arms	
Location of State of Bahia in Brazil	
Country	Brazil
Capital and Largest City	Salvador
Government	
- Governor	Jaques Wagner
- Vice Governor	Edmundo Pereira Santos
Area	
- Total	564692 km^2 (218028.8 sq mi)
Area rank	5th
Population (2005 census)	

- Total	13825883
- Estimate (2006)	13,950,146
- Rank	4th
- Density	24.5/km² (63.4/sq mi)
- Density rank	12th
Demonym	Baiano
GDP	
- Year	2006 estimate
- Total	R$ 96,559,000,000 (6th)
- Per capita	R$ 6,922 (19th)
HDI	
- Year	2005
- Category	0.742 – medium (18th)
Time zone	BRT (UTC-3)
- Summer (DST)	BRST (UTC-2)
Postal Code	40000-000 to 48990-000
ISO 3166 code	BR-BA
Website	bahia.ba.gov.br [1]

Bahia (Portuguese pronunciation: [ba'i.a]) is one of the 26 states of Brazil, and is located in the northeastern part of the country on the Atlantic coast.

It is the fourth most populous Brazilian state after São Paulo, Minas Gerais and Rio de Janeiro, and the fifth-largest in size. It is also one of the most important states in terms of history and culture in Brazil.

Bahia's capital is the city of Salvador, or more properly, São Salvador da Bahia de Todos os Santos, and is located at the junction of the Atlantic Ocean and the Bay of All Saints. The name "bahia" is an archaic spelling of the Portuguese word *baía*, meaning "bay", and comes from All Saints' Bay, first seen by European sailors in 1501.

Geography

The state's geographical regions comprise the Atlantic Forest. The *Recôncavo* region radiating from the Bay (the largest in Brazil), the site of sugar and tobacco cultivation. And the *Planalto*, which includes the fabled sertão region of Bahia's far interior. Bahia is bordered, in counterclockwise fashion, by Sergipe, Alagoas, Pernambuco and Piauí to the north, Goiás and Tocantins to the west, and Minas

Gerais and Espírito Santo to the south. The State of Bahia is crossed from north to south by a mountain chain which is marked, in the map, as Chapada Diamantina. This same chain receives other names, like Serra do Espinhaço, in Minas Gerais, and Borborema, in Pernambuco and Paraíba.

In some parts, the chain has the shape of "Chapadões", flat top plateaus with abrupt edges, the most visited of such chapadões are in the National Park of Chapada Diamantina, in the middle of the State. The chain divides Bahia in two clearly distinct geographical zones. To the east, where once existed the exuberant Atlantic Forest, the soil is fertile and, despite high temperatures, rainy seasons are regular.

The predominant vegetation in the west is "cerrado". These tough conditions caused the interior to be much less developed than the coast. The state is also crossed by the river São Francisco, the most important of Brazilian northeast. São Francisco River is a permanent river, which continuously supplies water to this arid region when many other smaller rivers dry out. The São Francisco starts in Minas Gerais and goes on until the Atlantic, making borders between Bahia and Alagoas. There are short stretches of the river which are navigable, but mainly for cargoes. The large blue spot at the north is a huge dam built to hold water for the hydroelectric plant of Itaparica.

Climate

Tropical. In addition to its considerable size, it has the longest coastline of the country: 1,103 km long (685 miles; north coast: 143; Todos os Santos Bay: 124; and southern: 418). With 68% of its territory located in the semi-arid zone, the State presents diversified climates and an average rainfall that varies from 363 to 2000 mm (14.3 to 79 in) per year, depending on the region. Regarding the weather, Bahia is one of the most privileged states of the country with the following temperatures: 19.2 to 26.6 °C (67 to 80 °F).

History

The Portuguese Pedro Álvares Cabral landed at what is now Porto Seguro City, on the southern coast of Bahia in 1500, and claimed the territory for Portugal. In 1549, Portugal established the city of Salvador, on a hill facing the Bay of All Saints. The city and surrounding captaincy served as the administrative and religious capital of Portugal's colonies in the Americas until 1763. The Dutch tried to hold control of Bahia but were defeated, only being able to seize Pernambuco. Charles Darwin visited Bahia in 1832 on his famous Voyage of The Beagle.

Historic Centre of Salvador.

The state was also the last area of Brazil to join the independent confederation. Some members in the elite remained loyal to the Portuguese crown after the rest of the country was granted independence.

After several battles, mostly in Pirajá, the province was finally able to expel the Portuguese on July 2, 1823, known as Bahia Independence Day, a great popular celebration. In the state there is an ongoing discussion about the exact moment of Brazilian independence, because for almost all baianos, it really happened in Bahia with the battles, and not on September 7, when the Emperor, Pedro I, declared independence.

Bahia was a center of sugar cultivation from the 16th to the 18th centuries, and contains a number of historic towns, such as Cachoeira, dating from this era. Integral to the sugar economy was the importation of a vast number of African slaves; more than 37% of all slaves taken from Africa were sent to Brazil, mostly to be processed in Bahia before being sent to work in plantations elsewhere in the country. The oldest Roman Catholic cathedral and the first medical college in the country are located in Bahia's capital, which also has one of the highest percentage of churches of any state capital in Brazil. The Catholic Archbishop of São Salvador da Bahia, Geraldo Majella Agnelo, is the Cardinal Primate of Brazil.

Demographics

See also: Largest Cities of Northeast Region, Brazil

According to the IBGE of 2008, there are 14,561,000 people residing in the state. The population density was 24.93 inhabitants per square kilometre (64.6 /sq mi).

Urbanization: 67.4% (2006); Population growth: 1.1% (1991–2000); Houses: 3,826,000 (2006).

The last PNAD (National Research for Sample of Domiciles) census revealed the following numbers: 9,149,000 Brown (Multiracial) people (62.83%), 3,000,000 White people (20.60%), 2,328,000 Black people (15.99%), 42,000 Amerindian people (0.29%), 37,000 Asian people (0.26%).

People in Bonfim Church. Religion in Bahia is a syncretic mix of European Catholicism and African religions.

City	Population
Salvador (the capital)	2,892,625
Feira de Santana	571,997
Vitória da Conquista	313,898
Juazeiro	230,538
Ilhéus	220,144
Itabuna	210,604

Jequié	145,964
Lauro de Freitas	144,492

Economy

The industrial sector is the largest component of GDP at 48.5%, followed by the service sector at 40.8%. Agriculture represents 10.7% of GDP (2004). Bahia exports: chemicals 22.4%, fuel 17.5%, mineral metallics 13%, paper 9.4%, cacao 5.6%, vehicles 4.8%, soybean 4.5% (2002).

Share of the Brazilian economy: 4.9% (2004).

The state has the biggest GDP of the states of the North/Northeast of Brazil. Bahia is the main producer and exporter of cacao in Brazil. In addition to important agricultural and industrial sectors, the state also has considerable mineral and petroleum deposits. In recent years, soy cultivation has increased substantially in the state. Bahia is the sixth largest economy of the country. In the mid 1950s, the Bahian economy could be considered a typical example of the primary-exporting model, which followed the subsistence production. For ten years this dynamic was led by cocoa crop that used to be the state's main product and its most important source of income.

With the acceleration of the industrialization process in the 70s', which started in the 50s, the productive structure began to change. This process, which was not limited to the regional market, was inserted in the Brazilian industry matrix through the chemical (specially petrochemical) and metallurgical segment. Consequently, for the last twenty years, the dynamism of the Bahian economy has surpassed the national economy and the State was able to present higher growth rates than the ones presented by the national economy. The industrial sector is expected to be the main contributor to this growth, particularly from 1999 on, when the investments that are being made now in the chemical, petrochemical and automotive segment, in agroindustry and food production will be consolidated.

The Bahian economy began 2005 in a very healthy state, with an exceptional trajectory of growth, once again presenting activity indicators superior to those of the Brazilian economy. Those numbers are the result of the endeavours of the Bahian Government, the result of increasing productive investment, and therefore, potential production, something that has been carried out through attractive enterprise policies in all segments of the economy, placing Bahia in a privileged position in the regional and national scenario. Today, the State has a differentiated economic profile, not just depending on one or two sectors. Bahian industry diversified and widened its productive base, with the implantation of new industrial segments, like the automobile and tyre industries, footwear and textile, furniture, food and beverages, cosmetics and perfumes, Information technology and naval.

Exceptional results can be seen in agriculture, commerce and tourism, where Bahia appears as one of the principle national destinies. For this to happen, the strategic position model of Bahia in the international tourism route was fundamental, with direct and regular flights to Europe, the United States, and the Southern Cone, due to the complementary governmental and private initiatives, besides the development of new tourist poles integrated to the local culture.

Chemical and Petrochemical

Bahia's Petrochemical Pole is the largest integrated complex in the Southern Hemisphere, and is the result of R$10 billion in investments, accounting for a third of the state's exports and for nearly half of the industrial production value.

Mining

Bahia is one of the richest states in minerals in the country, ranking third in Brazilian mineral production. The State's main products are gold, copper concentrate, magnesite, chromite, rock salt, barite, manganese, ornamental rocks, precious stones, talcum, phosphates and uranium.

Hydroelectric power plant in Sobradinho.

Automotive

In Bahia, the automotive sector has gained prominence since the creation of the Northeast Ford Complex in Camaçari (2001), and has become one of the most promising sectors of the Bahian economy. This enterprise, which was developed with the aim of generating 5,000 direct jobs and 55,000 indirect ones in 2005 has surpassed those expectations by creating 8,500 direct job positions and 85,000 indirect ones since its development.

Nowadays, Bahia produces about 10% of all vehicles produced in Brazil, occupying the third position in the national rankings. The Bahian automotive sector, led by Ford was in 2005 the third largest contributor (14.6%) to the Bahian GDP. It is important to highlight that Bahia had a 4.8% overall increase in its GDP, double the national performance, according to the Superintendency of Economic and Social Studies of Bahia (SEI)/Secretariat of Planning and IBGE.

Other Market Segments

Agribusiness; Footwear; Call Centers; Informatics, Electronics, and Telecommunications; Nautical; Paper and Pulp; Textiles; Plastic Transformation; and Tourism.

Tourism: Bahia's long coastline, beautiful beaches and cultural treasures make it one of Brazil's chief tourist destinations. In addition to the island of Itaparica, the town of Morro de São Paulo across the Bay on the northernmost tip of the southern coastline, and the large number of beaches between Ilhéus and Porto Seguro, on the southeastern coast, the littoral area north of Salvador, stretching towards the border with Sergipe, has become an important tourist destination. The *Costa do Sauípe* contains one of the largest resort hotel developments in Brazil and South America.

Regions of Bahia

The Coconut Coast

The Coconut Coast, in the northern of Bahia, corresponds to a total of 193 km (120 mi) of coast line, where coconut groves, dunes, rivers, swamps and sweet water lagoons are a constant scenario as well as the presence of the Atlantic Rain Forest. The Green Road, a road that connects Mangue Seco in the far north to Praia do Forte, crosses this beautiful region maintaining a critical distance from the areas of environmental preservation. For this reason the route is sometimes more than 10 km (6.2 mi) from the beach. At Praia do Forte, the road meets the Coconut Road (Estrada do Côco) and leads to Salvador, passing through spots, which are now integrated in the urban development of the state capital. In this region is located the Deputado Luís Eduardo Magalhães International Airport.

All Saints Bay

The largest bay on the Brazilian coast, Todos os Santos has a large number of islands with tropical beaches and vegetation. In its 1,052 square km, it contains 56 islands, receives sweet water from numerous rivers and creeks (especially the Paraguaçú and Subaé) and bathes the first capital of Brazil and the largest in the Northeast, Salvador, and more than ten municipalities. It is the largest navigable bay in Brazil and one of the most favorite spots for nautical sports, due to its regular breezes, medium annual temperature of 26 °C (79 °F) and sheltered waters. Todos os Santos Bay offers various leisure options, with hundreds of vessels of all different types, especially saveiros, schooners, motor boats, jet ski that criss-cross its crystalline waters on maritime excursions to the islands, and boat races. Major popular events and sport activities occur throughout the year, beginning on January 1, with the Procession of Bom Jesus dos Navegantes greeting the New Year.

Todos os Santos Bay has also been traditionally the venue for rowing contests at the Enseada dos Tainheiros, in Salvador, and now the bay is included in the routes of the great international regattas, such as the Ralley Les Iles du Soleil, regatta Hong Kong Challenge and the Expo 98 Round the World Ralley, which consider the bay an important stop along the route. The islands of the bay are a separate attraction. Some are privately owned, others were declared a state heritage and transformed into Environmental Protection Areas or ecological stations. Other islands are the patrimony of 12 municipalities located around the bay. Only a few are uninhabited and many have small communities where the natives live on fishing and tourism. All have common characteristics, such a calm sea, dense vegetation, especially coconuts and bananas, as well as vestiges of the Atlantic Forest. Of the 56 islands, the most important are Itaparica, Madre de Deus, Maré, Frades, Medo, Bom Jesus dos Passos.

Dendê Coast

The Dendê Coast, south of Salvador, is surrounded by verdant vegetation, clear waters, islands, bays, coral reefs and a very diversified fauna. It is connected to Salvador and the southern part of the state by ferryboats and the BA-001 highway, the second ecological highway along the Bahian coast, which connects the southern coastline and the extreme southern part of the state. It includes the municipalities of Valença, Cairu and the International attractions of Morro de São Paulo, Camamu, Taperoá, Ituberá and Maraú. The mouth of the Rio Una, in the form of a delta, contains 26 islands, the largest of which is Tinharé, where the Morro de São Paulo is located. At Boipeba and Cairú, which are part of the archipelago of Tinharé, the diversity of the ecosystems enables visitors to practice water sports, walk along the beach, follow trails in the rain forest and bathe on completely deserted beaches such as Garapuá.

Cacao Coast

Along the southern coast of Bahia, the Cacao Coast preserves ecological sanctuaries with dozens of kilometers of beaches shaded by dense coconut groves, the Atlantic Forest, large areas of wetland vegetation and cacao plantations, the great allies in the struggle to defend the preservation of the Atlantic Forest. Walking along paths in the forest or along the beaches, horseback riding along the coast, boat trips up the vast number of rivers are some of the options that the region offers. Here one can find Environmental Protection Areas at Itacaré/Serra Grande and the Lagoa Encantada in Ilhéus, the Biological Reserve of Una and the Ecological Reserve of Prainha at Itacaré. From the Morro de Pernambuco to Canavieiras, there are 110 km (68 mi) of beaches, some of them highly popular, and other deserted, with clear water, reefs, inlets, coconut grove and an infinite number of estuaries of rivers which extend throughout the Cacao Coast. Highway BA-001 links the municipalities, nearly always bordering the coastline. The most important locations at Cacao Coast are: Itacaré, Ilhéus, and Olivença.

The Discovery Coast

The Discovery Coast preserves, virtually intact, the landscape seen by the Portuguese fleet described in the first pages of the History of Brazil. There are approximately 150 km (93 mi) of beaches, inlets, bays, cliffs, numerous rivers and streams surrounded by the verdant coconut groves, wetlands and the Atlantic Forest. Over land and sea the excursions are always associated with nature, and there are various types of water sports, walks, trips on horseback, surfing and deep sea diving.

Church in Porto Seguro.

Recife de Fora, Coroa Alta and Trancoso for one day schooner excursions. BA-001 and two ferryboat systems over the Rio João de Tiba and Rio Buranhém connect the municipalities with the coast. Trips from Barra do Cai, passing through the Parque Nacional do Monte Pascoal, Caraíva, Trancoso, Arraial d'Ajuda, the environmental protection areas of Santo Antônio and Coroa Vermelha, to the mouth of the Rio João de Tiba as far as the Rio Jequitinhonha are among the various ecological trips for visitors.

The Whale Coast

Diving in the waters of the Abrolhos archipelago in the extreme southern part of Bahia is part of an ecotourist adventure. Whale watching is the preferred attraction of hundreds of tourists who arrive during the season of the "jubarte" whales, between July and November, when they migrate to Abrolhos. This region contains one of the largest concentrations of fish, in terms of volume and variety, per square meter on the planet. The underwater world contains a total of 17 species of corals that form an environment that is appropriate for numerous other species of maritime fauna. The Whale Coast includes the municipalities of Alcobaça, Caravelas, Nova Viçosa and Mucuri and its main attraction is the Parque Nacional Marino de Abrolhos.

The Diamantina Tableland Region

The geographical center of Bahia is the Diamantina Tableland region. In this mountainous region with a diversified topography, 90% of the rivers of the Paraguaçu, Jacuípe and Rio das Contas basins have their source here. There are thousands of kilometers of clear waters that spring from these mountains and descend in cascades and waterfalls to plateaus and plains, forming beautiful natural pools. The vegetation mixes cactus species of the caatinga dry lands with rare examples of the mountain flora, especially bromeliads, orchids and "sempre vivas" (member of the strawflower family). On the area one can find the three highest mountains in the state: Pico do Barbado, 2080 m (6820 ft) high, Pico Itobira, 1970 m (6460 ft), and Pico das Almas, 1958 m (6424 ft).

Chapada Diamantina.

Another scenic attraction is the Cachoeira da Fumaça (Waterfall), that falls 420 m (1380 ft), the Gruta dos Brejões, the largest cavern opening of Bahia, and the amazing Poço Encantado, which fascinates visitors to the region. There are so many natural attractions that it is possible to choose between subterranean routes in caves, or trip to waterfalls, trek along old gold mining trails or follow the steps of the Prestes Column, rapel, climb mountains, or go horseback riding in the Vale do Capão or Vale do Paty, in the midst of esoteric and alternative communities. Many of the sites are protected by the National Park of Diamantina Tableland region and the Environmental Preservation Area Serra do Barbado and Marimbus, Iraquara. There are opportunities to take long bikes, or travel on horseback, mountain bike or off-road vehicles.

Tourism and recreation

Bahia is the principal tourist center of the Northeast and 2nd of the country. The tourist product in Bahia, 50% of its global flow centered in Salvador, unites in a same space the characteristics of a natural landscape and a unique culture in the country, in which the typical culinary arts, the colonial architecture and popular feasts reveal a strong integration of elements of European and African origin in the formation and in the way of life of the people of Bahia. By its natural and historic-cultural attractions, Bahia presents an enormous potential for the development of the tourist activity. Owner of the biggest portion of seacoast of the country and of singular views in its interior, Bahia possesses specific cultural, folklore and religious characteristics, manifest in its extensive calendar of popular festivities, in its architectonic patrimony and in its typical food.

Salvador, with its Historical Center registered by UNESCO as Patrimony of Humanity and with its coast clipped into many beaches and dozens of islands, has a varied receptive infrastructure, composed of 170 hostelry units (of which 20 are of international standard hotels) and 25 thousand beds, further to restaurants, bars, nightclubs, shopping malls, theaters, crafts centers, Convention and Fairs Center, rental agencies, tourist agencies, and other equipment and services. In the last few years, the State Government promoted the total restoration of the Pelourinho, the biggest set of colonial style buildings in Latin America, today transformed into an important point for visitation by tourists, that will find there a synthesis of what best Bahia has to offer in specialized services, in regional and international cooking, in architecture of the 17th and 18th centuries and in music, with daily shows by the great artists of Bahia, famous in the country and abroad. The period of popular festivities in Bahia has its high point between December and March (summer months) and has in carnival its supreme point, with more than one million tourists in Salvador, Porto Seguro and other cities of the State's Tourist circuit.

Education

Educational institutions

- Universidade Federal da Bahia (UFBA) (Federal University of Bahia);
- Universidade Católica de Salvador [2] (UCSal) (Catholic University of Salvador);
- Centro Federal de Educação Tecnológica da Bahia [3] (Cefet-BA);
- Escola Baiana de Medicina e Saúde Pública [4] (EBMSP) (Bahiana School of Medicine and Public Health);
- Universidade Salvador [5] (Unifacs) (Salvador University);
- Universidade Federal do Recôncavo da Bahia [6] (UFRB) (Federal University of Recôncavo da Bahia);
- Universidade Estadual do Sudoeste da Bahia [7] (Uesb) (State University of Southwest of Bahia);

- Universidade Estadual de Santa Cruz [8] (UESC) (State University of Santa Cruz);
- Universidade do Estado da Bahia [9] (Uneb) (University of State of Bahia);
- Universidade Estadual de Feira de Santana [10] (UEFS) (State University of Feira de Santana);
- Fundação Universidade Federal do Vale do São Francisco [11] (UNIVASF) (Foundation Federal University of São Francisco Valley);
- Centro Universitário da Bahia [12] (FIB) (University Centre of Bahia);
- and many others.

Culture

As the chief locus of the early Brazilian slave trade, Bahia is considered to possess the greatest and most distinctive African imprint, in terms of culture and customs, in Brazil. These include the Yoruba-derived religious system of Candomblé, the martial art of capoeira, African-derived music such as samba (especially samba's Bahian precursor samba-de-roda), afoxé, and axé, and a cuisine with strong links to western Africa.

Capoeira in Salvador.

Bahia is the birthplace of many noted Brazilian artists, writers and musicians. Among the noted musical figures born in the state are Dorival Caymmi; João Gilberto; Gilberto Gil, the former (2003–2008) country's Minister of Culture; Caetano Veloso and his sister Maria Bethânia (Gil and Veloso being the founders of the Tropicália movement (a native adaptation of the hippie movement) of the late 1960s and early 1970s, which ultimate gained international recognition); Gal Costa; Luis Caldas; Sara Jane; Daniela Mercury; Ivete Sangalo; Carlinhos Brown and Margareth Menezes.

Nowadays, there are about 50 museums only in Salvador, of which 25 are functioning normally.

The city of Salvador is also home to famous groups known as "blocos-afros," including Olodum, Ara Ketu, É o Tchan, and Ilê Aiyê. Additionally, groups such as Chiclete com Banana also are based in Bahia. The first well-known rock'n roll singer in Brazil was also from Bahia. Born Raul Seixas, he was known as "Maluco Beleza" or "Peaceful Lunatic" (being "beleza (beauty)" in this manner means to be either "in peace" or "tranquil").

During the 19th century, one of Brazil's greatest poets, the Bahian abolitionist poet and playwright Castro Alves, a native of the *recôncavo* city of Cachoeira, penned his most famous poem, *Navio negreiro*, about slavery; the poem is considered a masterpiece of Brazilian Romanticism and a central anti-slavery text.

Other notable Bahian writers include Gregório de Matos, who wrote during the 17th century and was one of the first Brazilian writers, and Fr. Antonio Vieira, who during the colonial period was one of many authors who contributed to the expansion of the Portuguese language throughout the Brazilian territory.

The major Brazilian fiction writer of the 20th Century, Jorge Amado, was born in the southeastern Bahian city of Itabuna, and resided for many years in Salvador. His major novels include *Gabriela, Cinnamon and Cloves*; *Dona Flor and Her Two Husbands*; and *Tieta, the Goat Girl*, all of which became internationally renowned films. More recent writers from Bahia include the fiction writers João Ubaldo Ribeiro and Jean Wyllys, winner of Big Brother Brasil 5 in 2005. In the visual and plastic arts, one of the best known Bahian figures was the multigenre artist and Argentinian native Hector Julio Páride Bernabó, also known as Carybé (1911–1997). Fine examples of his work are visible in the Afro-Brazilian Museum in Salvador.

Carnival

Like river rapids, from which no one wants to escape, the 'Trio-Elétricos' sweep up whoever is in Salvador during Carnival. The 'Trio-Elétricos', floats with amplifiers used as moving stages, pass through three official circuits. Behind them, more than 2 million merrymakers dance along 25 km (16 mi) of streets and avenues. Osmar's float goes from Campo Grande to Castro Alves square, in the town centre; Dodô's float, goes from Farol da Barra to Ondina, along the coast; and Batatinha's float goes across the Pelourinho. The first is the oldest circuit. It is also where the event's most traditional groups parade. In the Dodô circuit, where the more famous artists' box seats are located, the party becomes lively toward the end of the afternoon, and it continues like this until morning.

Infrastructure

International airport

Deputado Luís Eduardo Magalhães International Airport is located in an area of more than 6 million square meters (1500 acres) between sand dunes and native vegetation. The road route to the airport has already become one of the city's main scenic attractions. And lies 20 km (12 mi) north of Downtown Salvador. In 2007, the airport handled 5,920,573 passengers and 91,043 aircraft movements, placing it 5th busiest airport in Brazil in terms of passengers. The airport's use has been growing at an average of 14% a year and now is responsible for more than 30% of passenger movement in Northeastern Brazil. Nearly 35 thousand people circulate daily through the passenger terminal. The airport generates more than 16 thousand direct and indirect jobs, to serve a daily average of over 10 thousand passengers, 250 takeoffs and landings of 100 domestic and 16 international flights.

There are good cafes and fast food restaurants at the airport. A bar offers alcoholic or soft drinks. There are several shops in the terminal building selling a variety of items, including fashion clothing, jewellery, gift items and books and magazines. There is also a pharmacy in the terminal building. Buses between the city centre and the airport are fairly frequent. Take the Praça da Sé (Sé Square)/Aeroporto bus. It is much cheaper than going by taxi. Buses also go to Rodoviária (Bus Terminal), which is the city's main bus station and located 5 km (3.1 mi) from the city centre. The car park of the airport, is located near the terminal building and has parking spaces for 600 cars.

The International Airlines are: Lufthansa, TAP, United Airlines, American Airlines, Alitália, Air France, Air Europa, Ibéria, Aerolíneas Argentinas, LanChile. In addition to domestic and regional services, the airport has non-stop flights to Lisbon, Madrid, Frankfurt, Montevideo, London, Santiago, Buenos Aires, Asunción and Miami. Its IATA airport code is SSA and it is the sixth busiest airport in the country, the first in northeastern Brazil, behind Congonhas International, Guarulhos International, Juscelino Kubitschek International, Santos Dumont Regional and Galeão International.

Highways

BA- 001,BR-101, BR-116, BR-242, BR-251, BR-324, BR-342, BR-367, BR-407, BR-418, BR-420, BR-445, BR-498.

Bahia's government is also inaugurating a large portion of the BA 001 between Morro de São Paulo and Itacare. The constructions began in September 2006 and it's scheduled to finish mid-2009. That portion of the highway will allow travelers to save up to two hours on a trip from Salvador to Ilheus or Itacare. It was a controversial part of the constructions since a small portion of native rain forest had to be destroyed. However, the IBAMA (Brazilian Institute of Environment and Renewable Natural Resources) followed closely the development of the road and the harm to the forest was minimal. The new part of the BA 001 will benefit thousands of families that live near the highway will be benefited with transportation, schools and will exponentially enhance tourism in Itacare, Camamu and Ilheus.

Linha Verde Highway.

The plan is to ultimately connect Bahia's coast from north to south entirely through BA-001.

Port

With cargo volume that grows year after year following the same economic development rhythm implemented in the State, the Port of Salvador, located in the Bahia de Todos os Santos, holds status as the port with the highest movement of containers of the North/Northeast and the second-leading fruit exporter in Brazil. The port's facilities operate from 8am to noon and from 1h30am to 5h30pm.

The ability to handle high shipping volume has positioned the port of Salvador for new investments in technological modernization, and the port is noted for implementing a high level of operational flexibility and competitive rates. The goal of port officials is to offer the necessary infrastructure for the movement of goods, while simultaneously meeting the needs of international importers and exporters.

Investments

The State of Bahia has been assigning a significant part of its revenues to public investments. The investment programs of the state have been backed basically by its own resources and, in a complementary fashion, with resources originating from credit operations signed with international organizations (World Bank, IDB, KFW, OECF, etc), and with national creditors (CEF, BNDES, etc). There are governmental investments in progress in the fields of environmental and urban sanitation (Bahia Azul), popular housing (Viver Melhor), transportation (Corredores Rodoviários), tourism (Prodetur), urban development (Produr), and regional development (Sertão Forte).

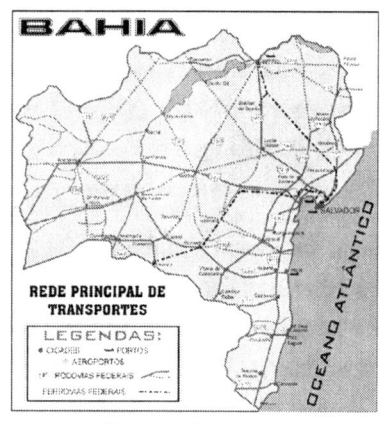

Transports in the state.

The airports of the State received special attention from the Government, with the development of a systematic program of reforms and improvements of the small airports of the interior, and, simultaneously, with the construction and/or improvements of the airports of the regions with some tourist appeal. Some distinction must be given in this work, for instance, to the construction of the airports of Piritiba and Mimoso do Oeste, in Barreiras region, both finished by now. To the landing runway and marshalling yard enlargements of the Porto Seguro Airport, enabling it to receive large aircrafts like the 767-400 Boeing. To the construction (in progress) of two new airports in the interior: one in Valença, near Morro de São Paulo, and the other in Lençóis, in the Diamantina Tableland region; also to some repairs and improvements of the airports of Jequié, Irecê, Barreiras, Feira de Santana and Esplanada, among many others.

The Government policy for transportation, has emphasized the integration of different transportation systems aiming to facilitate the flow of production, to reduce costs and to increase the competitiveness of the Bahian economy. For this purpose, the Government has conceived and is already implementing the "Corredor Intermodal de Transporte" (an intermodal transportation system), situated in the São Francisco River, that combines in one system waterways, roads and a railway. The system connects all the sailable part of the river (1371 km (852 mi) within the State) to many roads and to one railroad, the "Centro Atlântica". This system conducts to the Salvador and Aratu ports all the economic production of the West and São Francisco regions, at a reduced cost.

State University of Bahia in Caetité.

Social areas have also been given priority by current and previous administrations. The construction of new teaching facilities, the set up of a training and career development center for teachers, as well as new hospitals and health centers, and the acquisition of equipment and the modernization of the civil and military polices are examples of this Government's action. The significant increase in the amount of investments in the year 1997 is explained by the success of the state privatization program, confirming the purpose of the government in intensifying public development projects throughout the state. The State of Bahia has the best Human Development Index of Northeastern Brazil.

Sports

Football (*soccer* in the US) is the most popular sport. The two most popular football teams are Esporte Clube Bahia and Esporte Clube Vitoria . In 2008, Bahia plays in the Brazilian Championship Serie B (second division), while Vitoria plays in the Brazilian Championship Serie A (first division/premier league). Bahia has won the two most important football national league: The Taça Brasil in 1959 and the Brazilian Championship Serie A (Campeonato Brasileiro) in 1988. Bahia is also one of the original founders of the Thirteen's Club (some kind of special group that reunites the most important teams in the country). Vitoria has never been a national champion but was runner up of the Brazilian Serie A in 1993.

In the sport of boxing, Bahian native Acelino "Popó" Freitas is the current world champion (WBC) in the lightweight class.

Salvador is one of the host cities of the 2014 FIFA World Cup, for which Brazil is the host nation.

Further reading

- Anadelia A. Romo. *Brazil's Living Museum: Race, Reform, and Tradition in Bahia* (University of North Carolina Press; 2010) 221 pages; explores the shifting identity of the northeastern state of Bahia, which has a majority Afro-Brazilian population; covers the period from the abolition of slavery, in 1888, to the start of Brazil's military regime, in 1964.

External links

- (Portuguese) Official Website [13]
- (English) Brazilian Tourism Portal [14]
- (English) Bahia-Online.net [15]
- (English) Bahia Tourism [16]
- (Portuguese) History of Bahia [17]
- (Portuguese) Geography of Bahia [18]
- (Portuguese) Population of Bahia [19]

Samba

Samba	
Stylistic origins	Batuque Polka Maxixe Lundu Schottische Various urban styles of Brazilian music
Mainstream popularity	Brazil and widespread elsewhere
Subgenres	
Samba-canção, Partido alto, Samba-enredo, Samba de gafieira, Samba de breque, Bossa nova, Pagode	
Fusion genres	
Samba-maxixe, Samba-rock	
Other topics	
Brazilian Carnival, samba school	

Samba (Portuguese pronunciation: [ˈsẽbɐ] (listen)) is a Brazilian dance and musical genre originating in African roots. It is recognized around the world as a symbol of Brazil and the Brazilian Carnival. Considered one of the most popular Brazilian cultural expressions, together with Sertanejo, the samba has become an icon of Brazilian national identity. The Bahian *samba de roda* (dance circle), which became a UNESCO Heritage of Humanity in 2005, is the main root of the *samba carioca*, the samba that is played and danced in Rio de Janeiro.

Samba parade at Rio de Janeiro, 2008.

The modern samba that emerged at the beginning of the 20th century is basically 2/4 tempo and varied, with conscious use of the possibilities of chorus sung to the sound of palms and batucada rhythm, which adds one or more parts, or stanzas, of declaratory verses. Traditionally, the samba is played by strings (cavaquinho and various types of guitar) and various percussion instruments such as tamborim. By influence of American orchestras in vogue since the Second World War and the cultural impact of US music post-war, began to be used also as instruments trombones and trumpets, and the influence choro, flute and clarinet.

In addition to rhythm and bar set musically, historically brings in itself a whole culture of food (dishes for specific occasions), dances varied (miudinho, coco, samba de roda, pernada), parties, clothes (shoe nozzle fine, linen shirt, etc.), and the NAIF painting of established names such as Nelson Sargento, Guilherme de Brito and Heitor dos Prazeres, and anonymous artists community (painters, sculptors, designers and stylists) that makes the clothes, costumes, carnival floats and cars opens the wings of schools of samba.

The Samba National Day is celebrated on December 2. The date was established at the initiative of a Alderman of Salvador, Luis Monteiro da Costa, in honor of Ary Barroso, which was composed *"Na Baixa do Sapateiro"* - although he had never been in Bahia. Thus, on December 2 marked the first visit of the Ary Barroso to Salvador. Initially, this day was celebrated only in Salvador, but eventually turned into a national day.

Samba is a root style on Southeastern Brazil and Northeast Brazil, specially in Rio de Janeiro , Sao Paulo and Salvador (also Axé on Northeast), but it has a minor importance in Southern Brazil, Center-West Brazil and all countryside Brazil where Sertanejo is the most popular music style .

History

Background

Origins of the word samba

Although samba exists throughout the big, multiraced country—especially in the states of Bahia, Maranhão, Minas Gerais, and São Paulo—in the form of various popular rhythms and dances that originated from the regional batuque, a type of music and associated dance form from Cape Verde, the samba is a particular musical expression of urban Rio de Janeiro, where it was born and developed between the end of the 19th century and the first years of the 20th. It was in Rio that the dance practiced by former slaves who migrated from

The Batuque (music)Batuque practiced in Brazil of the 19th century, in a painting by Johann Moritz Rugendas.

Candy land in the northeast came into contact and incorporated other genres played in the city (such as the polka, the maxixe, the lundu, and the xote, among others), acquiring a completely unique character

and creating the *samba carioca urbana* (samba school) and *carnavalesco* (Carnaval school director). In reality, the samba schools are large organizations of up to 5000 people which compete annually in the

Carnival with thematic floats, elaborate costumes and original music.

During the first decade of the 20th century, some songs under the name of samba were recorded, but these recordings did not achieve great popularity. However, in 1917 *"Pelo Telefone"* ("By Phone") was recorded, which is considered the first true samba. The song was claimed to be authored by Ernesto dos Santos, best known as DongaWikipedia:WikiProject Disambiguation/Fixing links, with co-composition attributed to Mauro de Almeida, a well-known Carnaval columnist. Actually, "Pelo Telefone" was created by a collective of musicians who participated in celebrations at the house of Tia Ciata (Aunt Ciata); it was eventually registered by Donga and the Almeida National Library.

"Pelo Telefone" was the first composition to achieve great success with the style of samba and to contribute to the dissemination and popularization of the genre. From that moment, samba started to spread across the country, initially associated with Carnival and then developing its own place in the music market. There were many composers such as Heitor dos Prazeres, João da Bahiana, Pixinguinha and Sinhô, but the sambas of these composers were "amaxixados" (a mix of maxixe), known as sambas-maxixes.

The contours of the modern samba came only at the end of the 1920s, from the innovations of a group of composers of carnival blocks in the neighborhoods of Estácio de Sá and Osvaldo Cruz, and the hills of Mangueira, Salgueiro and São Carlos. Since then, there have been many great names in samba, such as Ismael Silva, Cartola, Ary Barroso, Noel Rosa, Ataulfo Alves, Wilson Batista, Geraldo Pereira, Zé Kéti, Candeia, Ciro Monteiro, Nelson Cavaquinho, Elton Medeiros, Paulinho da Viola, Martinho da Vila, and many others.

As the samba consolidated as an urban and modern expression, it began to be played on radio stations, spreading across the hills and neighborhoods to the affluent southern areas of Rio de Janeiro. Initially viewed with prejudice and discriminated against because of its black roots, the samba, because of its hypnotic rhythms and melodic intonations, as well as its playful lyrics, eventually conquered the white middle class as well. Derived from samba, other musical genres earned themselves names such as samba-canção, partido alto, samba-enredo, samba de gafieira, samba de breque, bossa nova, samba-rock, pagode, and many others. In 2007, the IPHAN turned the into a Samba a Cultural Heritage of Brazil.

The samba is frequently associated abroad with the football and Carnival. This history began with the international success of "Aquarela do Brasil," by Ary Barroso, followed with Carmen Miranda (supported by Getúlio Vargas government and the US Good Neighbor policy), which led to the samba United States, went further by bossa nova, which finally entered the country in the world of music. The success of the samba in Europe and Japan only confirms its ability to win fans, regardless of language. Currently, there are hundreds of samba schools held on European soil (scattered by countries like Germany, Belgium, Netherlands, France, Sweden, Switzerland). Already in Japan, the records invest heavily in the launch of former Sambistas set of discs, which eventually create a market comprised solely of catalogs of Japanese record labels.

There are several versions about the birth of the word *"samba"*. One of them claims to be from the words *"Zambra"* or *"Zamba"*, come from Arabic, having been born more precisely when invasion of the Moors to Iberian Peninsula in the 8th century. Another says it is originating from one of many African languages, possibly the Kimbundu, where *"sam"* means *"give"* and *"ba"* means *"receive"* or *"thing falls"*.

In Brazil, folklorists suggest that the word *"samba"* is a corruption of the Kikongo word *"Semba"*, translated as "umbigada" in Portuguese, meaning "a blow struck with the belly button".

One of the oldest records of the word samba appeared in magazine's Pernambuco *O Carapuceiro*, dated February 1838, when Father Miguel Lopes Gama of Sacramento wrote against what he called the *"samba d'almocreve"* - not referring to future musical genre, but a kind of merriment (dance drama) popular for blacks of that time. According to Hiram Araújo da Costa over the centuries, the festival of dances of slaves in Bahia were called *"samba"*.

In the middle of the 19th century, the word samba defined different types of music made by African slaves, when conducted by different types of Batuque, but assumed its own characteristics in each Brazilian states, not only by the diversity of tribes for slaves, and the peculiarity of each region in which they were settlers. Some of these popular dances were known: bate-baú, samba-corrido, samba-de-roda, samba-de-Chave and samba-de-barravento in Bahia; coco in Ceará; tambor-de-crioula (or ponga) in Maranhão; trocada, coco-de-parelha, samba de coco and soco-travado in Pernambuco; bambelô in Rio Grande do Norte; partido-alto, miudinho, jongo and caxambu in Rio de Janeiro; samba-lenço, samba-rural, tiririca, miudinho and jongo in São Paulo.

Favela and Tias Baianas

From the second half of the 19th century, as people black and mestiza in Rio de Janeiro - from various parts of the Brazil, mainly in Bahia, as well as ex-soldiers of War of Canudos the end of that century - grew, these people the vicinity of Morro da Conceição, Pedra do Sal, Praça Mauá, Praça Onze, Cidade Nova, Saúde and Zona Portuária. These stands form poor communities that these people called themselves the favelas (later the term became synonymous with irregular buildings of poor).

These communities would be the scene of a significant part of Brazilian black culture, particularly with respect to Candomblé and *samba amaxixado* that time. Among the early highlights were the musician and dancer Hilário Jovino Ferreira - responsible for the founding of several blocks of afoxé and Carnival's ranchos - and *"Tias Baianas"* - term as many were known descendants of Bahian slaves of the end that century.

Among the main *"Tias Baianas"*, highlight the Tia Amelia (mother of DongaWikipedia:WikiProject Disambiguation/Fixing links), Tia Bebiana, Tia Monica (mother of Pendengo and Carmen Xibuca), Tia Prisciliana (mother of João da Bahiana), Tia Rosa Olé, Tia Sadata, Tia Veridiana (mother of Chico da Baiana). Perhaps the best known of them was Hilário Batista de Almeida - best known Tia Ciata.

Thus, as the samba and musical genre born in the houses of *"Tias Baianas"* (Bahian aunts) in beginning of the 20th century, as a descendant of the style lundu of the candomblé de terreiro parties between umbigada (Samba) and capoeira's pernadas, marked in pandeiro, prato-e-faca (plate-and-knife) and in and the palm of the hand. There are some controversies about the word *samba-raiado*, one of the first appointments to the samba. It is known that the *samba-raiado* is marked by the sound and accent sertanejos / rural brought by *"Tias Baianas"* to Rio de Janeiro. According to João da Baiana, the *samba-raiado* was the same as *chula raiada* or samba de partido-alto. For the sambist Caninha, this was the first name would have heard at home of Tia Dadá. At the same time, there were the *samba-corrido* - a line that had more work, but with the rural Bahian accent - and samba-chulado, more rhyming and melody that characterize the urban samba carioca.

Scenes in Bahia and São Paulo

The urban carioca samba is the anchor of 20th century *"Brazilian samba"* par excellence. However, before this type of samba was to consolidate as the *"national samba"* in Brazil, there were traditional forms of sambas in Bahia and São Paulo.

The rural Bahia samba acquired additional names as choreographic variations - for example, the *"samba-de-chave"*, where the soloist dancer faking looking wheel in the middle of a key, and when found, was replaced. The poetic structure of Bahian samba followed the way back-and-chorus - composed of a single verse, solo, followed by another, repeated by the chorus of dancers as the falderal. No chorus, the samba is called *samba-corrido*, variant uncommon. The chants were taken by one singer, one of the musicians or soloist dancer. Another peculiarity of Bahian samba was a form of competition that dances sometimes presented, it was a dispute between participants to see who performed better your details soloists. Besides the umbigada, common to all the bahianian samba, the Bahia presented three basic steps: *corta-a-joca*, *separa-o-visgo* and *apanha-o-bag*. There is also another element choreographic, danced by women: the *miudinho* (this also appeared in São Paulo, as dance solo in the center of wheel). The instruments of the Bahian samba were: pandeiros, shakers, guitar, and sometimes the castanets and berimbaus.

In São Paulo state, samba became the domain black to caboclo. And in rural area, can provide without the traditional umbigada. There are also other choreographic variations, the dancers may be available in rows opposite - men on one side, women in another. The instruments of the samba paulista were: violas, adufes e pandeiros. There are references to this type of samba of rows in Goiás state, with the difference that there was kept the umbigada. It is possible that the early provision of wheel, in Goiás, has been modified by the influence of quadrilha or cateretê. According to historian Luís da Câmara Cascudo, it is possible to observe the influence of city in the samba, by the fact that it is also danced by pair connections.

The first decades of the 20th century

"Pelo Telefone"

Grandmother of the composer Bucy Moreira, Tia Ciata was responsible for the sedimentation of samba carioca. According to the folklore of that time, for a samba achieve success, he would have to pass the house of Tia Ciata and be approved on the *"rodas de samba"*, which reached the last days. Many compositions were created and sung in improvisation, where the samba *"Pelo Telefone"* (from DongaWikipedia:WikiProject Disambiguation/Fixing links and Mauro de Almeida), samba for which there were also many other versions, but to come to the history of Brazilian music as the first samba to be recorded in 1917.

Meanwhile other recordings have been recorded as samba before *"Pelo Telefone"*, this composition was done by double Donga / Mauro de Almeida who is regarded as founder of the genus in March. Still, the song is written and discussed its proximity to the maxixe made it finally designated as samba-maxixe. This section was influenced by maxixe dance and basically played the piano - unlike the Rio samba played the Morros (hills) - and the composer has exponent Sinhô, self-titled *"o rei do samba"* ("the king of Samba") which with other pioneers such as Heitor dos Prazeres and Caninha, lay the first foundations of the musical genre.

Turma do Estácio

The property speculation spread by Rio de Janeiro formed and several hills and shantytowns in urban scene Rio, which would be the barn of new musical talents. Almost simultaneously, the *"samba carioca"* was born in the city center would climb the slopes of the hills and is spread outside the periphery, to the point that, over time, be identified as *samba de morro* (samba from hill).

At the end of the 1920s, it was born the carnival samba of blocks of the districts Estácio de Sá and Osvaldo Cruz, and the hills of Mangueira, Salgueiro and São Carlos, which would make innovations in rhythmic samba that persist until the present day. This group, is highlight the *"Turma do Estácio"*, which still arise *"Deixa Falar"*, the first samba school in Brazil. Formed by some composers in the neighborhood of Estácio, including Alcebíades Barcellos (aka Bide) Armando Marçal, Ismael Silva, Nilton Bastos and the more "malandros" as Baiaco, Brancura, Mano Edgar, Mano Rubem, the *"Turma do Estácio"* marked the history of the Brazilian samba by injecting more pace to the genus one perforated, which has endorsement of youth's middle class, as the ex-student of law BarrosoWikipedia:WikiProject Disambiguation/Fixing links and former student of medicine Noel Rosa.

Initially a "rancho carnavalesco", then a Carnival's Block and finally, a samba school, the *"Deixa Falar"* was the first to Rio Carnival parade in the sound of an orchestra made up of percussion surdos, tambourines and cuícas, who joined pandeiro and shakers. This group was instrumental called *"bateria"* and lends itself to the monitoring of a type of samba that was quite different from those of

Donga, Sinhô and Pixinguinha. The samba of Estácio de Sá signed up quickly as the samba carioca par excellence.

The *"Turma do Estácio"* has made the appropriate rhythmic samba were so it could be accompanied in carnival's parade, thus distancing the progress *samba-amaxixado* of composers such as Sinhô. Moreover, its wheels of samba were attended by composers from other Rio hills, as Cartola, Carlos Cachaça and then Nelson Cavaquinho e Geraldo Pereira, Paulo da Portela, Alcides Malandro Histórico, Manacéia, Chico Santana, and others. Accompanied by a pandeiro, a tambourine, a cuíca and a surdo, they created and spread the samba-de-morro.

Popularization in the 1930's and 1940's

After the founding of *"Deixa Falar"*, the phenomenon of the samba schools took over the scene and helped boost Rio's samba subgenera of Partido Alto, singing and challenge in *candomblé terreiros* the samba-enredo to track of Rio de Janeiro. carnival parades.

From the 1930s, the popularization of radio in Brazil helped to spread the samba across the country, mainly the sub-genres *samba-canção* and *samba-exaltação*. The *samba-canção* was released in 1928 with the recording *"Ai, yo-yo"* by Aracy Cortes. Also known as samba half of the year, the *samba-canção* has become established in the next decade. It was a slow and rhythmic samba music and had an emphasis on melody and generally easy acceptance. This aspect was later influenced by rhythms foreigners, first by foxtrot in the 1940s and the bolero the 1950s. Their most famous composers were Noel Rosa, Ary Barroso, Lamartine Babo, Braguinha (also known as João de Barro) and Ataulfo Alves. Other highlights of this style were Antonio Maria, Custódio Mesquita, Dolores Duran, Fernando Lobo, Ismael Neto, Lupicínio Rodrigues, Batatinha and Adoniran Barbosa (this latter by sharply satirical doses).

The ideology of Getúlio Vargas's Estado Novo contaminated the scene of the samba, beside the *samba-exaltação*. With *"Aquarela do Brasil"*, composed by Ary Barroso and recorded by Francisco Alves in 1939, the *samba-exaltação* had become the first success abroad. This kind of samba was characterized by extensive compositions of melody and patriotic verses. Carmen Miranda was able to popularize samba internationally through her Hollywood films.

With the support of the Brazilian president Getúlio Vargas, the samba won status the "official music" of Brazil. But this status of national identity also came the recognition of intellectual Heitor Villa-Lobos, who arranged a recording with the maestro Leopold Stokowski in 1940, which involved Cartola, DongaWikipedia:WikiProject Disambiguation/Fixing links, João da Baiana, Pixinguinha and Zé da Zilda.

Also in the 1940s, there arose a new crop of artists: Francisco Alves, Mário Reis, Orlando Silva, Silvio Caldas, Aracy de Almeida, Dalva de Oliveira, and Elizeth Cardoso, among others. Others such as Assis Valente, Ataulfo Alves, Dorival Caymmi, Herivelto Martins, Pedro Caetano, and Synval Silva led the samba to the music industry.

A new beat in the 1950's: the Bossa Nova

A movement was born in the south area of Rio de Janeiro and strongly influenced by jazz, marking the history of samba and Brazilian popular music in the 1950s. The bossa nova emerged at the end of that decade, with an original rhythmic accent—which divided the phrasing of the samba and added influences of impressionist music and jazz—and a different style of singing, intimate and gentle. After precursors as Johnny Alf, João Donato and musicians as Luis Bonfá and Garoto, this sub-genre was inaugurated by João Gilberto, Tom Jobim and Vinicius de Moraes, and would have a generation of disciples, followers and Carlos Lyra, Roberto Menescal, Durval Ferreira and groups as Tamba Trio, Bossa 3, Zimbo Trio and The Cariocas.

The sambalanço also began at the end of the 1950s. It was a branch of the popular bossa nova (most appreciated by the middle class) which also mingled samba rhythms and American jazz. Sambalanço was often found at suburban dances of 1960s, 1970s and 1980s. This style was developed by artists such as Bebeto, Bedeu, Scotland 7, Djalma Ferreira, the Daydreams, Dhema, Ed Lincoln, Elza Soares, and Miltinho, among others. In the 21st century, groups such as Funk Como Le Gusta and Clube do Balanço continue to keep this sub-genre alive.

Rediscovered of the samba's roots in the 1960s and 1970s

In the 1960s, Brazil became politically divided with the arrival of a military dictatorship, and the leftist musicians of bossa nova started to gather attention to the music made in the *favelas*. Many popular artists were discovered at this time. Names like Cartola, Nelson Cavaquinho & Guilherme de Brito, Velha Guarda da Portela, Zé Keti, and Clementina de Jesus recorded their first albums.

In the 1970s, samba returned strongly to the air waves with composers and singers like Paulinho da Viola, Martinho da Vila, Clara Nunes, and Beth Carvalho dominating the hit parade. Great samba lyricists like Paulo César Pinheiro (especially in the praised partnership with João Nogueira) and Aldir Blanc started to appear around that time.

Rapprochement with the hill

With bossa nova, samba is further away from its popular roots. The influence of jazz is deepened and techniques have been incorporated classical music. From a festival in Carnegie Hall of New York, in 1962, the bossa nova reached worldwide success. But over the 1960s and 1970s, many artists who emerged—like Chico Buarque, Billy Blanco, Martinho da Vila and Paulinho da Viola—advocated the return of the samba beat its traditional, with the return of veterans as Candeia, Cartola, Nelson Cavaquinho e Zé Kéti. In the early the 1960s was the *"Movement for Revitalization of Traditional Samba"*, promoted by Center for Popular Culture, in partnership with the Brazilian National Union of Students. It was the time of the appearance of the bar Zicartola of the samba shows at the Teatro de Arena and the Teatro Santa Rosa and musical as *"Rosa de Ouro"*. Produced by Herminio Bello de Carvalho, the "Rosa de Ouro" revealed Araci Cortes and Clementina de Jesus. During the sixties, some samba groups appeared and formed by previous experiences with the world of samba and songs recorded by great names of Brazilian music. Among them were The Cinco Crioulos, The Voz do Morro, Mensageiros do Samba and The Cinco Só.

By that time, emerged a dissent within the bossa nova with *afro-sambas*, by Baden Powell and Vinicius de Moraes. Moreover, the movement approached traditional sambistas revised the samba of the hill, especially Cartola, Elton Medeiros, Nelson Cavaquinho, Zé Kéti and further Candeia, Monarco, Monsueto and Paulinho da Viola. Following the steps of Paulo da Portela, that intermediate the relationship of the hill with the city where the samba was pursued, Paulinho da Viola—also the Portela samba school—would be a sort of ambassador of traditional gender before a more public art, including the tropicalists. Also within the bossa nova appears Jorge Ben; his contribution to merge with American rhythm and blues, which would further the emergence of a subgenus called *swing* (or *samba-rock*).

Outside the main scene of the so-called Brazilian Popular Music festivals, the sambists found the Bienal do Samba, in the late sixties, the space for the big names of the genus and followers. Even in the final decade, came the so-called *samba-empolgação* 'samba-excitement' of carnival blocks *Bafo da Onça, Cacique de Ramos,* and *Boêmios de Irajá*.

A fusion: the samba-funk

Also in the 1960s, came the samba funk. The samba-funk emerged at the end of the 1960s with pianist Dom Salvador and its group, which merge the samba with American funk newly arrived in the Brazilian lands. With the final journey of Dom Salvador for United States, the band closed the business, but at the beginning of 1970s some ex-members as hit Luiz Carlos, José Carlos Barroso and Oberdan joined Christopher Magalhaes Bastos, Jamil Joanes, Cláudio Lúcio da Silva Stevenson and to form Banda Black Rio. The new group has deepened the work of Don Salvador in the binary mixture of the bar with the Brazilian samba funk of the American Quaternary, based on the dynamics of implementation, driven by drums and bass. Even after the Banda Black Rio in 1980s, British djs began to disclose the group's work was rediscovered and pace throughout the Europe, mainly in UK and Germany.

Partido-Alto for the masses

At the turn of the 1960s to the 1970s, the young Martinho da Vila would give a new face to the traditional sambas-enredo established by authors such as Silas de Oliveira and Mano Decio da Viola, compressing them and expanding its potential in the music market. Furthermore, Martin popularize the style of the Partido alto (with songs like *"Casa de Bamba"* and *"Pequeno Burguês"*), launched on its first album in 1969.

Although the term arose in the beginning of century in Tia Ciata house (initially to describe instrumental music), the term *partido alto* came to be used to signify a type of samba which is characterized by a highly percussive beat of pandeiro, using the palm of the hand in the center of the instrument in place. The harmony of Partido alto is always higher in pitch, usually played by a set of percussion (usually surdo, pandeiro, and tambourine) and accompanied by a cavaquinho and/or a guitar. But from this high-assimilated by the record industry was made of written soil, and no more spontaneous and improvised, according to traditional canons.

Also in that decade, some popular singers and composers appeared in the samba, as Alcione, Beth Carvalho, Clara Nunes. As highlighted in city of São Paulo, Geraldo Filme was one of the leading names in samba paulistano, next to Germano Mathias, Osvaldinho of Cuíca, Tobias da Vai-Vai, Aldo Bueno, and Adoniran Barbosa; this latter has duly recognized nationally before being recalled and rewritten more often in the seventies.

1980s until 1990s

In the early 1980s, after having been eclipsed by the popularity of disco and Brazilian rock, Samba reappeared in the media with a musical movement created in the suburbs of Rio de Janeiro. It was the *pagode*, a renewed samba, with new instruments—like the banjo and the tan-tan—and a new language that reflected the way that many people actually spoke with the inclusion of heavy *gíria* (slang). The most popular artists were Zeca Pagodinho, Almir Guineto, Grupo Fundo de Quintal, Jorge Aragão, and Jovelina Pérola Negra.

In 1995, the world saw come out from Savador one of the moust popular Pagode group, the Gera Samba, later renamed É o Tchan. This group created the most sexual dannce of the Pagode from 1990s, a music with a strange like. Some groups like Patrulha do Samba and Harmonia do Samba, also mixtured a bit of Axé. Samba, as a result, morphed during this period, embracing types of music that were growing popular in the Caribbean such as rap, reggae, and rock. Examples of Samba fusions with popular Caribbean music is samba-rap, samba-rock and samba-reggae, all of which were efforts to not only entertain, but to unify all Blacks throughout the Americas culturally and politically, through song. In other words, samba-rap and the like, often carried lyrics that encouraged Black pride, and spoke out against social injustices. Samba, however, is not accepted by all as the national music of Brazil, or as a valuable art form. What appears to be new is the local response flow, in that instead of simply assimilating outside influences into a local genre or movement, the presence of

Zeca Pagodinho, one of popular contemporany sambists.

foreign genres is acknowledged as part of the local scene: samba-rock, samba-rap. But this acknowledgment does not imply mere imitation of the foreign models or, for that matter, passive consumption by national audiences. Light-skinned, "upper-class," Brazilians often associated Samba with dark-skinned blacks because of its arrival from West Africa. As a result, there are some light-skinned Brazilians who claim that samba is the music of low-class, dark-skinned Brazilians and, therefore, is a "thing of bums and bandits."

Samba continued to act as a unifying agent during the 1990s, when Rio stood as a national Brazilian symbol. Even though it was not the capital city, Rio acted as a Brazilian unifier, and the fact that samba originated in Rio helped the unification process. In 1994, the World Cup had its own samba composed for the occasion, "Copa 94." The 1994 FIFA World Cup, in which samba played a major cultural role, holds the record for highest attendance in World Cup history. Samba is thought to be able to unify because individuals participate in it regardless of social or ethnic group. Today, samba is viewed as perhaps the only uniting factor in a country fragmented by political division .

The Afro-Brazilians played a significant role in the development of the samba over time. This change in the samba was an integral part of Brazilian nationalism, which was called "Brazilianism".

> "What appears to be new is the local response to that flow, in that instead of simply assimilating outside influences into a local genre or movement, the presence of foreign genres is acknowledged as part of the local scene: samba-rock, samba-reggae, samba-rap. But this acknowledgment does not imply mere imitation of the foreign models or, for that matter, passive consumption by national audiences." — Gerard Béhague Selected Reports in Ethnomusicology) Pg. 84

Samba in the 21st century

From year 2000, there were some artists who were looking to reconnect most popular traditions of samba. Were the cases of Marquinhos of Oswaldo Cruz, Teresa Cristina among others, that contributed to the revitalization of the region of Lapa, in the Rio de Janeiro. In São Paulo, samba resumed the tradition with concerts in Sesc Pompéia Club and also by the work of several groups, including the group Quinteto em Branco e Preto who developed the event "Pagode da Vela" ("Pagoda of Sail"). This all helped to attract many artists from Rio de Janeiro, who shows, established residence in neighborhoods of the capital paulistana.

In 2004, the minister of culture Gilberto Gil submitted to the Unesco the application of damping off of samba as Cultural Heritage of Humanity in category "Intangible Goods" by Institute of National Historical and Artistic Heritage. In the following year, the samba-de-roda of Baiano Recôncavo was proclaimed part of the Heritage of Humanity by Unesco, in the category of "Oral and intangible expressions."

In 2007, IPHAN gave the official record, the Book of Registration of Forms of Expression, the matrices of the samba of Rio de Janeiro: *samba de terreiro, partido-alto* e *samba-enredo*.Samba (

pronunciation (help·info)) is a Brazilian dance and musical genre originating in African and European roots. The word is derived from the Portuguese verb sambar, meaning "to dance to rhythm." It is a worldwide recognized symbol of Brazil and the Carnival and is the national dance of Brazil. Considered one of the most popular Brazilian cultural expressions, the samba has become an icon of Brazilian national identity.[1][2][3] The Bahian samba de roda (dance circle), which became a UNESCO Heritage of Humanity in 2005, was a basis of the samba carioca, the samba that is played and danced in Rio de Janeiro.

Although samba exists throughout the country—especially in the states of Bahia, Maranhão, Minas Gerais, and São Paulo—in the form of various popular rhythms and dances that originated from the regional batuque, a type of music and associated dance form from Cape Verde, the samba is a particular musical expression of urban Rio de Janeiro, where it was born and developed between the end of the 19th century and the first decades of the 20th century. It was in Rio that the dance practiced by former slaves who migrated from Bahia in the northeast came into contact and incorporated other genres played in the city (such as the polka, the maxixe, the lundu, and the xote, among others), acquiring a completely unique character and creating the samba carioca urbana (samba school) and carnavalesco (Carnaval school director).[3] In reality, the samba schools are large organizations of up to 5000 people which compete annually in the Carnival with thematic floats, elaborate costumes and original music.

During the 1910s, some songs under the name of samba were recorded, but these recordings did not achieve great popularity; however, in 1917, was recorded in disc "Pelo Telefone" ("By Phone"), which is considered the first samba. The song has the authority claimed by Ernesto dos Santos, best known as Donga, with co-authors attributed to Mauro de Almeida, a known carnaval columnist. Actually, "Pelo Telefone" was creating a collective of musicians who participated in the celebrations of the house Tia Ciata (Ciata aunt), but eventually registed by Donga and the Almeida National Library.[3]

"Pelo Telefone" was the first composition to achieve success with the brand of samba and contribute to the dissemination and popularization of the genre. From that moment, samba started to spread across the country, initially associated with Carnival and then buying a place in the music market. There were many composers as Heitor dos Prazeres, João da Bahia, Pixinguinha and Sinhô, but the sambas of these composers were "amaxixados" (a mix of maxixe), known as sambas-maxixes.[3]

The contours of the modern samba came only at the end of the 1920s, from the innovations of a group of composers of carnival blocks of neighborhoods of Estácio de Sá and Osvaldo Cruz, and the hills of Mangueira, Salgueiro and São Carlos. Since then, there were great names in samba, and some as Ismael Silva, Cartola, Ary Barroso, Noel Rosa, Ataulfo Alves, Wilson Batista, Geraldo Pereira, Zé Kéti, Candeia, Ciro Monteiro, Nelson Cavaquinho, Elton Medeiros, Paulinho da Viola, Martinho da Vila, and many others.[3]

As the samba is consolidated as an urban and modern expression, he began to be played in radio stations, spreading the hills and neighborhoods to south area of Rio de Janeiro. Initially viewed with prejudice and criminalized by their black backgrounds, the samba to conquer the public middle class as well. Derived from samba, other musical earned themselves names such as samba-canção, partido alto, samba-enredo, samba de gafieira, samba de breque, bossa nova, samba-rock, pagode, and many others. In 2007, the IPHAN became the Samba a Cultural Heritage of Brazil.[3]

The samba is the most popular musical genre in Brazil, well known associated abroad with the football and Carnival. This history began with the international success of "Aquarela do Brasil," by Ary Barroso, followed with Carmen Miranda (supported by Getúlio Vargas government and the US Good Neighbor policy), which led to the samba United States, went further by bossa nova, which finally entered the country in the world of music. The success of the samba in Europe and Japan only confirms its ability to win fans, regardless of language. Currently, there are hundreds of samba schools held on European soil (scattered by countries like Germany, Belgium, Netherlands, France, Sweden, Switzerland). Already in Japan, the records invest heavily in the launch of former Sambistas set of discs, which eventually create a market comprised solely of catalogs of Japanese record labels.[3]

The modern samba that emerged from the beginning of the century rate is basically 2/4 tempo and varied, with conscious use of the possibilities of chorus sung to the sound of palms and batucada rhythm, and which would add one or more parts, or offices of declamatory verses. Traditionally, the samba is played by strings (cavaquinho and various types of guitar) and various percussion instruments such as tambourine. By influence of American orchestras in vogue since the Second World War and the cultural impact of US music post-war, began to be used also as instruments trombones and trumpets, and the influence choro, flute and clarinet.

In addition to rhythm and bar set musically, historically brings in itself a whole culture of food (dishes for specific occasions), dances varied ((miudinho, coco, samba de roda, pernada), parties, clothes (shoe nozzle fine, linen shirt, etc.), and the NAIF painting of established names such as Nelson Sargento, Guilherme de Brito and Heitor dos Prazeres, and anonymous artists community (painters, sculptors, designers and stylists) that makes the clothes, costumes, carnival floats and cars opens the wings of schools of samba.

The Samba National Day is celebrated on December 2. The date was established at the initiative of a Alderman of Salvador, Luis Monteiro da Costa, in honor of Ary Barroso, which was composed "Na Baixa do Sapateiro" - although he had never been in Bahia. Thus, on December 2 marked the first visit of the Ary Barroso Salvador. Initially, this day was celebrated only Samba in Salvador, but eventually turned into a national day.

Instruments of a Samba band

Basics

- chocalho
- reco-reco
- Cavaquinho
- Guitar
- Pandeiro
- Surdo
- Tamborin
- Tantã
- Repinique/Repique
- Snare Drum/Caixa/Tarol
- Ago-go
- Ganza/Chocalho

Others

- Cuíca
- Trumpet

See also

- List of Brazilian musicians#Samba
- List of English words of African origin

References

- *The Brazilian Sound: Samba, Bossa Nova and the Popular Music of Brazil.* by McGowan, Chris and Pessanha, Ricardo. 2nd edition. Temple University Press. 1998.
- *Samba on Your Feet* [1] by Eduardo Montes-Bradley documentary on the history of samba in Brazil with particular emphasis on Rio de Janeiro. The film is in Portuguese with English subtitles and approaches the subject from an interesting perspective.

External links

- Origins of Samba Dance & Music [2]
- All Brazilian Music samba page [3]
- One of the first formal samba definition (1997) [4]
- Loronix [5] is the largest virtual community around the Brazilian music on the Internet.
- Dance Samba Spain (Madrid) - www.andreabrasilmadrid.es. [6]
- Samba from the Favelas [7], some podcasts from 'RadioFavela - The Sound of Rio'
- Die Samba Show [8] ISWC T-0425394804 "Latin Complete Collection" Album. *Published with the permission of the owner of rights*

pnb:سمبا

Capoeira

Capoeira or the Dance of War by Johann Moritz Rugendas, 1825, published in 1835

Also known as	'Dance of War'
Focus	Acrobatics Kicking Striking Takedowns Leg Sweeps
Country of origin	Brazil Afro-Brazilian
Famous practitioners	Manuel dos Reis Machado (Mestre Bimba) Vicente Ferreira Pastinha João Grande João Pereira dos Santos (Mestre João Pequeno) Reinaldo Ramos Suassuna Rildo Cordeiro (Mestre Penteado) Bira Almeida (Mestre Acordeon) José Tadeu Carneiro Cardoso (Mestre Camisa) Anderson Silva Lateef Crowder Eddy Gordo (fictional character) Bradley Mayhew L Lawliet (fictional character) Sanji (Fictional character)

Capoeira (Portuguese pronunciation: [kapuˈejɾe]) is an Afro-Brazilian art form that combines elements of martial arts, music, and dance. It was created in Brazil by African slaves by mixing the many fighting styles from many of their tribes, sometime after the sixteenth century. It was developed in the region of Quilombo dos Palmares, located in the Brazilian state of Alagoas, which was the state of Pernambuco before dismemberment, and has had great influence on Afro-Brazilian generations, with strong presence in the states of Bahia, Pernambuco, Rio de Janeiro and São Paulo. Participants form a *roda*, or circle, and take turns either playing musical instruments (such as the Berimbau), singing, or ritually sparring in pairs in the center of the circle. The sparring is marked by fluid acrobatic play, feints, takedowns, and with extensive use of leg sweeps, kicks, and headbutts. Less frequently used techniques include elbow strikes, slaps, punches, and body throws. Its origins and purpose are a matter of debate, with theories ranging from views of Capoeira as a uniquely Brazilian folk dance with improvised fighting movements to claims that it is a battle-ready fighting form directly descended from ancient African techniques.

Etymology

The word "capoeira" had a probable origin as a derisive term used by slave owners to refer to its practice as chicken fights (the word literally means "chicken coop" in Portuguese). Another claim is that the word "capoeira" derives from the Native-American language Tupi-Guarani words *kaá* ("leaf", "plant") and *puéra* (past aspect marker), meaning "formerly a forest."[citation needed]

Afro-Brazilian art form

Capoeira is a direct descendant of African fighting styles, and was incorporated with Brazilian dance form distilled from African slaves in Brazil which is in essence from various African and Brazilian influences. One popular explanation holds that it is an African fighting style that was developed in Brazil, as expressed by a proponent named Salvano,Wikipedia:Avoid weasel words who said, "Capoeira cannot exist without black men but its birthplace is Brazil... Capoeira, as it was taught to me, is the warrior's dance that was done between slaves that escaped their masters outside the cities. I was taught Capoeira in Rio de Janeiro by master Morcego who had come from Bahia, where he said Capoeira was played in the streets since he was little." (Page' Retifumo, MR)[citation needed]

Some interpretations emphasize capoeira as a fighting style designed for rebellion, but disguised by a façade of dance. Supporting the martial interpretation are renderings in the 1835 *Voyage Pittoresque dans le Brésil* (*Picturesque Voyage to Brazil*), where ethnographic artist Johann Moritz Rugendas depicts *Capoeira or the Dance of War*, lending historical credence to the idea that Capoeira is a combative art form with many dance elements.

Other Pan African-American combative traditions parallel capoeira. According to Dr. Morton Marks, the island of Martinique is famous for danymé, also known as ladja. As with capoeira, "there is a ring of spectators into which each contestant enters, moving in a counter-clockwise direction and dancing toward drummers. This move, known as *Kouwi Lawon* (or 'Circular Run' in Creole), is an exact parallel to the capoeira interlude called *dá volta ao mundo* or 'take a turn around the world.'" Marks stated that in Cuba, a mock-combat dance called Mani was performed to yuka drums. "A dancer (manisero) would stand in the middle of a ring of spectator-participants and, moving to the sound of the songs and drums, would pick someone from the circle and attempt to knock them down." Some of the manisero's moves and kicks were similar to those of Afro-Brazilian capoeira including its basic leg-sweep (rasteira).

In *Capoeira : A History of an Afro-Brazilian Martial Art*, Matthias Röhrig Assunção compared "three American combat traditions: knocking and kicking in the United States, *ladija* in Martinique, and capoeira in Brazil." African-derived combat games similar to wrestling and stick fighting were also witnessed and documented in 17th-century Barbados, 18th-century Jamaica, and 19th century Venezuela. Stick fighting was and still is practiced in Trinidad, Carriacou, Dominica, and Haiti.

Maya Talmon-Chvaicer suggested capoeira may have been influenced by a ritual fight-dance called N'golo (the zebra dance) from Southern Angola, which was performed during the "Efundula, a puberty rite for women of the Mucope, Muxilenge, and Muhumbe tribes of southern Angola." Since the 1960s, the N'golo theory has become popular amongst some practitioners of capoeira Angola, although it is not universally accepted.

While many of these games are combative, it is widely accepted that slaves in the New World would have sought both violent and jovial means of coping with their oppression.

Status in Brazil and development as a sport

For some time, Capoeira was criminalized and prohibited in Brazil. Assunção provided ample data from police records dating back to the 1800s demonstrating that capoeira was an "important reason" to detain slaves and "free coloured individuals". "From 288 slaves that entered the Calabouço jail during the year 1857-1858, 80 (31 per cent) were arrested for [capoeira], and only 28 (10.7 per cent) for running away. Out of 4,303 arrests in Rio police jail in 1862, 404 detainess --nearly 10 per cent-- had been arrested for capoeira." In 1890, Brazilian president Deodoro da Fonseca signed an act that prohibited the practice of capoeira nationwide, with severe punishment for those caught.[citation needed] It was nevertheless practiced by the poorer population on public holidays, during work-free hours, and on other similar occasions. Riots, also caused by police interference, were common[citation needed].

In spite of the ban, Manuel dos Reis Machado (Mestre Bimba) pioneered academic capoeira which became knowns as "Capoeira Regional." Reis Machado was finally successful in convincing the authorities of the cultural value of capoeira, thus ending the official ban in the 1930s. Reis Machado founded the first capoeira school in 1932, the Academia-escola de Capoeira Regional at the Engenho de Brotas in Salvador-Bahia. He was then considered "the father of modern capoeira". In 1937, he earned the state board of education certificate. In 1942, Reis Machado opened his second school at the Terreiro de Jesus - rua das Laranjeiras. The school is still open today and supervised by his pupil, known as "Vermelho-27"[citation needed].

Having saved capoeira from illegality, Mestre Bimba began being challenged by other capoeira masters who possessed their own unique capoeira styles, such as capoeira *angola*. There were several prominent *angola* mestres at this time in Salvador and they held regular *rodas* together in an area called Gengibirra of Salvador. There were twenty-two mestres in all; among them were *Mestre*

Amorzinho—who commanded the *rodas*--, Daniel Coutinho--"Mestre Noronha"--, Onça Preta, Geraldo Chapeleiro, Juvenal, and Livino Diogo. Together they founded a center for capoeira Angola. Around the time of Amorzinho's death in 1941-1942 Vicente Ferreira Pastinha, best known as "*Mestre Pastinha*", took over the center, called the *Centro Esportivo de Capoeira Angola*. Pastinha worked almost up to his death in 1981 to codify the more traditional Angola style of capoeira and he wrote endlessly on the sport. Because he preserved much of the traditional style of capoeira, in his practice, teachings, and writings, he too is important to modern capoeira.

UFC Middleweight Champion Anderson Silva is a practitioner of Capoeira.

Outside Brazil

"Artur Emídio was probably the first capoeirista ever to perform abroad;" in the late 1950s and early 1960s he went to Argentina, Mexico, the US, and Europe. Groups such as Brazil Tropical, headed by Domingos Campos and M. Camisa Roxa, toured Europe in the 1970s. Jelon Vieira's Dance Brazil, founded in New York City in 1977, has been particularly influential in popularizing the capoeira among American audiences.

In the mid-1970s masters of the art form began to emigrate and teach capoeira in the United States and other countries. At this time capoeira in Brazil was still primarily practiced among the poorest and blackest of Brazilians. With its immigration to the U.S., however, much of the stigma with which it was historically associated in Brazil was shed.

Today there are many capoeira schools all over the world, and it has attracted a broad spectrum of multicultural, multiracial students.[*citation needed*]

Music

Main article: Capoeira music

Music is integral to capoeira. It sets the tempo and style of game that is to be played within the *roda*. The music is composed of instruments and song. The tempos differ from very slow (*Angola*) to very fast (*são bento regional*). Many of the songs are sung in a call and response format while others are in the form of a narrative. Capoeiristas sing about a wide variety of subjects. Some songs are about history or stories of famous capoeiristas. Other songs attempt to inspire players to play better. Some songs are about what is going on within the roda. Sometimes the songs are about life or love lost. Others

A capoeira bateria led by Cobra Mansa featuring three berimbaus and a pandeiro.

have lighthearted and playful lyrics. Capoeiristas change their playing style significantly as the songs or rhythm from the berimbau commands. In this manner, it is truly the music that drives capoeira.

There are three basic kinds of songs in capoeira[citation needed]. A *ladainha* (litany) is a narrative solo usually sung at the beginning of a roda, often by the *mestre* (master). These ladainhas will often be famous songs previously written by a mestre, or they may be improvised on the spot. A ladainha is usually followed by a *chula* or *louvação*, following a call and response pattern that usually thanks God and one's teacher, among other things. Each call is usually repeated word-for-word by the responders. The ladainha and chula are often omitted in regional games. Finally, *corridos* are songs that are sung while a game is being played, again following the call and response pattern. The responses to each call do not simply repeat what was said, however, but change depending on the song.

The instruments are played in a row called the bateria. The rhythm of the bateria is set by the berimbaus (stringed percussion instruments that look like musical bows). Other instruments in the bateria are: two *pandeiros* (tambourines), a *reco-reco* (rasp), and an *agogô* (double gong bell). The atabaque (conga-like drum), a common feature in most capoeira baterias, is considered an optional instrument, and is not required for a full bateria in some groups.

Ranks

While the variety in styles lead to a variety of ranking systems, there is a standard trend that most systems of capoeira follow. In order of ascension, those ranks are *aluno* (student), *graduado* (graduated), *formado* (formed), *professor* (teacher), and *mestre* (master).

Usually at their first *batizado* (baptism), a capoeirista will be given the rank of *aluno*. In some styles, this may also come with a *cordão* (rope) and / or *apelido* (nickname). *Aluno* translates to "student" in English, and so an *aluno* is a student of capoeira. Their rank is a recognition of their readiness to learn.

After an *aluno* becomes well versed in the capoeira they are learning, they can be recognized as an *aluno graduado* (graduated student). This means they've learned enough about capoeira to be trusted to teach the art to others. At this point, they would continue to learn not only capoeira, but how to teach capoeira. It could be considered the equivalent of a black belt in Eastern martial arts.

An *aluno graduado* can then become an *aluno formado* (formed student). They have formed their own capoeira and are now ready to teach others. A *formado* will usually be an instructor assisting the head of whichever school they are a part of.

The *aluno formado* goes on to become a *professor*. *Formado* and *professor* are generally similar in rank, the main difference being a professor might have his own school in which to teach, while a *formado* would usually be an assistant instructor.

The final rank in capoeira would be a *mestre* (master). As the name states, the mestre is a master of capoeira. *Mestres* tend to be the true voices of capoeira. All other ranks are usually assigned by a *mestre*, but this rank is hard to assign. For the most part, a capoeirista becomes a *mestre* when the capoeira community recognizes them as one. This will usually take place after 15 to 20 years of continuous training.

The jogo (game/match)

See also: List of capoeira techniques

Capoeira does not focus on injuring the opponent. Rather, it emphasizes skill. Capoeiristas often prefer to show the movement without completing it though it could be finished to cause harm to the receiver, enforcing their superiority in the roda. If an opponent cannot dodge a slow attack, there is no reason to use a faster one. Each attack that comes in gives players a chance to practice an evasive technique.

Capoeiristas outside

Ginga

The *ginga* (literally: rocking back and forth; to swing) is the fundamental movement in capoeira. Capoeira Angola and Capoeira Regional have distinctive forms of *ginga*. Both are accomplished by maintaining both feet approximately shoulder-width apart and then moving one foot backwards and then back to the base, describing a triangular step on the ground. This movement is done to prepare the body for other movements.

The rest of the body is also involved in the *ginga*: coordination of the arms (in such a way as to prevent the body from being kicked), torso (many core muscles may be engaged depending on the player's style), and the leaning of the body (forward and back in relation to the position of the feet; the body leans back to avoid kicks, and forward to create opportunities to show attacks). The overall movement should match the rhythm being played by the *bateria*.

Attacks

Capoeira primarily attacks with kicks, sweeps, takedowns, and head strikes. Some schools teach punches and hand strikes, but they are not as common. A possible explanation for the primary use of feet is the common West African belief that hands are for creation and feet for destruction[citation needed]. Another common explanation is that slaves in Brazil were commonly shackled at the wrists, restricting them from using their hands[citation needed]. Lastly, striking with the hands is often seen as inelegant and disruptive to the flow of the game. Elbow strikes are commonly used in place of hand strikes. "Cabeçadas" or headbutts are as common as they are in many of the fighting arts of the African Diaspora[citation needed]. Knee strikes are sometimes seen. Capoeira also uses acrobatic and athletic movements to maneuver around the opponent. Cartwheels called "*aú*" (a very common acrobatic movement), handstands (*bananeira*), headspins (*pião de cabeça*), hand-spins (*pião de mão*), handsprings (*gato*), sitting movements, turns, jumps, flips (*mortal*), and large dodges are all very common in capoeira though vary greatly depending on the form and rhythm. Fakes and feints are also an extremely important element in capoeira games. The setting of traps or illusory movements are very common.

Defenses

Capoeira defenses consists of evasive moves and rolls. A series of ducks called *esquivas*, which literally means "escape", are also staple of a capoeiristas' defensive vocabulary. There are typically different esquivas for every step of the Ginga, depending on the direction of the kick and intention of the defender. A common defense is the *rolê*, which is a rolling move that combines a duck and a low movement. This move allows the defensive players to quickly evade an attack and position themselves around the aggressor in order to lay up for an attack. It is this combination of attacks and defense which gives a game of capoeira its perceived 'fluidity' and choreography.

Other evasive moves such as *rasteira*, *vingativa*, *tesoura de mão* or *queda* allow the capoeirista to move away or dangerously close in an attempt to trip up the aggressor in the briefest moment of vulnerability (usually in a mid-kick.)

Combinations

There are also styles of moves that combine both elements of attack and defense. An example is the *au batido*. The move begins as an evasive cartwheel which then turns into a blocking/kick, either as a reflexive response to a blocking move from the opposing player or when an opportunity to do so presents itself, e.g., at an opponent's drop of guard. Two kicks called *meia-lua-de-frente* and *armada* are often combined to create a double spinning kick.

A Capoeira movement (Aú Fechado) (click for animation).

Chamada

The Chamada is a ritual that takes place within the game of Capoeira Angola. Chamada means 'call', and consists of one player 'calling' their opponent to participate in the ritual. There is an understood dialogue of gestures of the body that are used to call the opponent, and to signal the end of the ritual. The ritual consists of one player signaling, or calling the opponent, who then approaches the player and meets the player to walk side by side within the roda. The player who initiated the ritual then decides when to signal an end to the ritual, whereby the two players return to normal play. The critical points of the chamada occur during the approach, and the chamada is considered a 'life lesson', communicating the fact that the approach is a dangerous situation. Approaching people, animals, or life situations is always a critical moment when one must be aware of the danger of the situation. The purpose of the chamada is to communicate this lesson, and to enhance the awareness of people participating in the ritual.

During the ritual, after the opposing player has appropriately approached the caller of the chamada, the players walk side by side inside the circle in which the game is played. This is another critical situation, because both players are now very vulnerable due to the close proximity and potential for surprise attack.

Experienced practitioners and masters of the art will sometimes test a student's awareness by suggesting strikes, head-butts, or trips during a chamada to demonstrate when the student left themselves open to attack. The end of a chamada is called by the player that initiated the ritual, and consists of a gesture inviting the player to return to normal play. This is another critical moment when both players are vulnerable to surprise attack.

The chamada can result in a highly developed sense of awareness and helps practitioners learn the subtleties of anticipating another person's intentions. The chamada can be very simple, consisting solely of the basic elements, or the ritual can be quite elaborate including a competitive dialogue of trickery, or even theatric embellishments.

Volta ao mundo

Volta ao mundo means "around the world".

The volta ao mundo takes place after an exchange of movements has reached a conclusion, or after there has been a disruption in the harmony of the game. In either of these situations, one player will begin walking around the perimeter of the circle, and the other player will join the "around the world" before returning to the normal game.

Malandragem

Malandragem is a word that comes from malandro, which means a person who possesses cunning as well as malicia, which translates to "malice." This, however, is misleading as the meaning of malicia means trickery/deceit. The word comes from the historical folklore of Brasil, in which men who were marginalized from main stream society and possessed street smarts were called malandros. Malandragem is an attitude derived from the mindset of the malandro and is a unique and distinguishing characteristic of the art of capoeira.

Capoeira angola

Main article: Capoeira Angola

Capoeira angola is considered to be the more ancient form of capoeira[citation needed] and is often characterized by deeply held traditions, slower movements and with the players playing their games in closer proximity to each other than in regional or contemporanea. Capoeira angola is often characterized as being slower and lower to the ground than other major forms of Capoeira, although in actual practice, the speed varies in accordance with the music. It is played much as it Capoeira originally was played on the street before being moved indoors and systematized into the more modernized version of Capoeira regional. Capoeira Angola is also known for the *chamada*, a physical call-and-response used to challenge an opponent or to change the style in the roda.

The father of the best known modern Capoeira angola schools is considered to be Grão-Mestre Pastinha who lived in Salvador, Bahia. Today, many of the Capoeira angola schools in the United States come from Mestres in Pastinha's lineage. He was not the only Capoeira angola mestre, but is considered to be the "Father of Capoeira angola" bringing this style of Capoeira into the modern setting of an academy. He also wrote the first book about Capoeira, Capoeira Angola, now out of print. Capoeira angola has experienced an explosion of growth during the past 20 years, it can be found in few cities Brazil where it's not often practiced or even recognized as real capoeira and many larger cities in the USA, Europe, South America, Japan, as well as many other locations.

Capoeira regional

Regional is the more common form of Capoeira, it is practiced much more widely in Brazil then any other style of Capoeira and it's often what Brazilians refer to when they speak of Capoeira. Capoeira Regional was developed by Reis Machado (Mestre Bimba) to make capoeira more effective and bring it closer to its fighting origins, and less associated with the criminal elements of Brazil. The Capoeira Regional style is often considered to consist of faster and more athletic play than the lesser-known Capoeira angola.

Later, *modern regional* came to be Capoeira Contemporânea. Developed by other people from Bimba's regional, this type of game is characterized by high jumps, acrobatics, and spinning kicks. This *regional* should not be confused with the original style created by Reis Machado.

Regional ranks capoeiristas by ability, denoting different skill with the use of a *corda* (colored rope, also known as *cordel* or *cordão*) worn as a belt. Angola does not use such a formal system of ranking, relying instead upon the discretion of a student's mestre. In both forms, though, recognition of advanced skill comes only after many years of constant practice[citation needed].

Capoeira Contemporânea

Contemporânea is a term for groups that train multiple styles of capoeira simultaneously. Very often students of Capoeira Contemporânea train elements of Regional and Angola as well as newer movements that would not fall under either of those styles.

The label Contemporânea also applies to many groups who do not trace their lineage through Reis Machado or Pastinha and do not strongly associate with either tradition.

In recent years, the various philosophies of modern capoeira have been expressed by the formation of schools, particularly in North America, which focus on and continue to develop their specific form of the modern art. This has become a defining characteristic of many schools, to the point that a seasoned student can sometimes tell what school a person trains from, based solely on the way they play the game. Some schools teach a blended version of the many different styles. Traditionally, rodas in these schools will begin with a period of Angola, in which the school's mestre, or an advanced student, will sing a ladainha, (a long, melancholy song, often heard at the start of an Angola game). After some time, the game will eventually increase in tempo, until, at the mestre's signal, the toque of the berimbaus changes to that of traditional Regional.

Each game, Regional and Angola stresses different strengths and abilities. Regional emphasizes speed and quick reflexes, whereas Angola underscores a great deal of thought given to each move, almost like a game of chess. Schools that teach a blend of these try to offer this mix as a way of using the strengths of both games to influence a player.

Special events

Capoeira regional groups periodically hold *Batizados* ("baptisms" into the art of capoeira). Members being "baptized" are normally given a *corda* (cord belt) and an *apelido* (capoeira nickname) if they haven't already earned one. *Batizados* are major events to which a number of groups and masters from near and far are normally invited.

Sometimes a *Batizado* is also held in conjunction with a *Troca de Corda* (change of belts), in which students already baptized who have trained hard and been deemed worthy by their teachers are awarded higher-ranking belts as an acknowledgment of their efforts. Such ceremonies provide opportunities to see a variety of different capoeira styles, watch *mestres* play, and see some of the best of the game.

Batizados and *Trocas de Cordoes* do not occur in capoeira Angola, which does not have a system of belts. However, some contemporary schools of capoeira have combined the study of both arts and may require their students to be learned in the ways of capoeira Angola before being awarded a higher belt.

Related activities

Samba de roda

Main article: Samba

Performed by many capoeira groups, samba de roda is a traditional Afro-Brazilian dance & musical form that has been associated with capoeira for many years. The orchestra is composed by pandeiro (tambourine), atabaque (drum), berimbau-viola (berimbau with the smallest cabaça and the highest pitch), chocalho (rattle − a percussion instrument), accompanied by singing and clapping. Samba de roda is considered the primitive form of modern Samba.

Maculelê

Main article: Maculelê (dance)

Maculelê is a dance that tells the story of the enslaved Africans who worked the sugarcane plantations in Brasil. The sugar cane was cut with machetes, and in the Maculele dance, dancers click machete blades rhythmically within the dance. Sometimes sticks are used instead of machete blades, however it is understood the sticks symbolize the machetes used to cut the sugarcane in the time of slavery. Maculele and capoeira share the same history and tell the story of the people who invented these art forms, therefore they are usually taught and performed together.

Puxada de rede

Main article: Puxada de rede

Puxada de Rede is a Brazilian folkloric theatrical play, seen in many capoeira performances. It is based on a traditional Brazilian legend involving the loss of a fisherman in a sea-faring accident

Important mestres

See also: Category:Capoeira mestres

- Manuel dos Reis Machado (Mestre Bimba), a founder of the Luta Regional Bahiana.
- Vicente Ferreira Pastinha (Mestre Pastinha), a founder of the Centro Esportivo Capoeira Angola.
- Reinaldo Ramos Suassuna (*Mestre Suassuna*), a founder of "Cordao de Ouro."
- Mestre Besouro Mangangá
- Mestre João Grande
- Mestre João Pequeno
- Mestre Mark Terakedis

See also

- List of capoeira techniques
- Capoeira in popular culture
- Capoeira music
- Capoeira toques
- Malicia
- CapoeirArab

Notes

Printed references

- Assunção, Matthias Röhrig (2005). *Capoeira : A History of an Afro-Brazilian Martial Art*. New York: Routledge. ISBN 0-7146-8086-9.
- Capoeira, Nestor (2003). *The Little Capoeira Book*. (Alex Ladd, Trans.). Berkeley: North Atlantic. ISBN 1-55643-440-5.
- Talmon-Chvaicer, Maya (2007). *The Hidden History of Capoeira: A Collision of Cultures in the Brazilian Battle Dance*. ISBN 978-0-292-71723-7.

Further reading

- Almeida, Birra "Mestre Acordeon" (1986). *Capoeira: A Brazilian Art Form*. Berkeley: North Atlantic Books. ISBN 0-938190-30-X.
- Merrell, Floyd (2005). *Capoeira and Candomblé: Conformity and Resistance in Brazil*. Princeton: Markus Wiener. ISBN 1-55876-349-X.

External links

- Capoeira [1] at the Open Directory Project
- Grupo Nzinga de Capoeira Angola: Grupo Nzinga [2]
- Rio Janeiro Capoeira [3]

A free, educational podcast in English and Portuguese on the topic Capoeira (interviews with various Mestres from multiple schools) is available at CapoeiraPod [4]

Overview of Salvador

Salvador, Bahia

Salvador da Bahia
— Municipality —
The Municipality of São Salvador da Bahia de Todos os Santos
Flag Seal
Nickname(s): *Capital da Alegria* (Capital of happiness) and *Roma Negra* (Black Rome).
Motto: *Sic illa ad arcam reversa est* (And thus the dove returned to the ark)
Location of Salvador in the State of Bahia

	Salvador da Bahia
Location in Brazil	
Coordinates: 12°58′29″S 38°28′36″W	
Country	Brazil
Region	Northeast
State	Bahia
Founded	March 29, 1549
Government	
- Mayor	João Henrique Carneiro (PMDB)
Area	
- Municipality	706 km^2 (272.6 sq mi)
Elevation	8 m (26 ft)
Population (2009)	
- Municipality	2998096 (3rd)
- Density	4176.6/km^2 (10817.3/sq mi)
- Metro	3866004
Time zone	UTC-3
Postal Code	40000-000
Area code(s)	+55 71
HDI (2000)	0.805 – high
Website	Salvador, Bahia [1]

Salvador da Bahia (Portuguese pronunciation: [sawvaˈdoɾ], *Savior*; historic name: **São Salvador da Bahia de Todos os Santos**, in English: "Holy Savior of All Saints' Bay") is a largest-city on the northeast coast of Brazil and the capital of the Northeastern Brazilian state of Bahia. Salvador is also known as

Brazil's capital of happiness due to its easygoing population and countless popular outdoor parties, including its street carnival. The first colonial capital of Brazil, the city is one of the oldest in the country and in the New World. For a long time, it was simply known as **Bahia**, and appears under that name (or as *Salvador da Bahia, Salvador of Bahia* so as to differentiate it from other Brazilian cities of the same name) on many maps and books from before the mid-20th century. Salvador is the third most populous Brazilian city, after São Paulo and Rio de Janeiro, and it is the ninth most populous city in Latin America.

The city of Salvador is notable in Brazil for its cuisine, music and architecture, and its metropolitan area is the wealthiest in Brazil's Northeast, its poorest region. Over 80% of the population of metropolitan region of Salvador has Black African ancestry, the African influence in many cultural aspects of the city makes it the center of Afro-Brazilian culture and this reflects in turn a curious situation in which African-associated cultural practices are celebrated, but Black Bahians due to their low income are apart from most of the city life options. The historical center of Salvador, frequently called the Pelourinho, is renowned for its Portuguese colonial architecture with historical monuments dating from the 17th through the 19th centuries and has been declared a World Heritage Site by UNESCO in 1985.

Salvador is located on a small, roughly triangular peninsula that separates Todos os Santos Bay from the open waters of the Atlantic Ocean. The bay, which gets its name from having been discovered on All Saints' Day forms a natural harbor. Salvador is a major export port, lying at the heart of the *Recôncavo Baiano*, a rich agricultural and industrial region encompassing the northern portion of coastal Bahia. The local terrain is diverse ranging from flat to rolling to hills and low mountains.

A particularly notable feature is the escarpment that divides Salvador into the *Cidade Alta* ("Upper Town" - rest of the city) and the *Cidade Baixa* ("Lower Town" - northwest region of the city), the former some 85 m (279 ft) above the latter, with the city's cathedral and most administrative buildings standing on the higher ground. An elevator (the first installed in Brazil), known as *Elevador Lacerda*, has connected the two sections since 1873, having since undergone several upgrades.

The Deputado Luís Eduardo Magalhães International Airport connects Salvador with Brazilian cities and also operates international flights, and the city is home to the Federal University of Bahia.

History

Baía de Todos os Santos (All Saints Bay) was first encountered by the Portuguese and named in 1502. In 1501, one year after the arrival of Pedro Álvares Cabral's fleet in Porto Seguro, Gaspar de Lemos arrived at Todos os Santos Bay and sailed most of the Bahia coast. But the first European man to disembark on "Morro de São Paulo," Saint Paul's Mount, was Martim Afonso de Sousa, in 1531, leading an expedition to explore the coast of the new continent. In 1510, a ship, containing the Portuguese settler named Caramuru by the natives, wrecked near the borough of Rio Vermelho. In 1534, Francisco Pereira Coutinho founded a town near Barra borough, called *Vila Velha*, Portuguese for "Old Village."

In 1549, a fleet of Portuguese settlers headed by Tomé de Sousa, the first Governor-General of Brazil, established Salvador. Built on a high cliff overlooking All Saints bay as the first colonial capital of colonial Brazil, it quickly became its main sea port and an important center of the sugar industry and the slave trade. Salvador was divided into an upper and a lower city, the upper one being the administrative and religious area and where the majority of the population lived. The lower city was the financial center, with a port and market. In the late 19th Century, funiculars and an elevator, the *Elevador Lacerda*, were built to link the two areas.

Campo Grande Square.

The city became the seat of the first Catholic bishopric of Brazil in 1552, and is still a center of Brazilian Catholicism. By 1583, there were 1,600 people residing in the city, and it quickly grew into one of the largest cities in the New World, surpassing any colonial American city at the time of the American Revolution in 1776. Salvador was the capital city of the Portuguese viceroyalty of Grão-Pará and its province of Bahia de Todos os Santos. The Dutch Republic captured and sacked the city in May of 1624, and held it along with other north east ports until it was retaken by a Spanish-Portuguese fleet in May 1625. It then played a strategically vital role in the Portuguese-Brazilian resistance against the Dutch.

Salvador was the first capital of Brazil and remained so until 1763, when it was succeeded by Rio de Janeiro. The city became a base for the Brazilian independence movement and was attacked by Portuguese troops in 1812, before being liberated on July 2, 1823. It settled into graceful decline over the next 150 years, out of the mainstream of Brazilian industrialization. It remains, however, a national cultural and tourist center. By 1948 the city had some 340,000 people, and was already Brazil's fourth largest city. In 2008 was 2,948,733, the third largest population of Brazil.

In the 1990s, a major city project cleaned up and restored the old downtown area, the *Pelourinho*, or *Centro Historico* ("Historical Center"). Now, the Pelourinho is a cultural center, and the heart of Salvador's tourist trade. Nonetheless, this social prophylaxis resulted in the forced removal of thousands of working class residents to the city's periphery where they have encountered significant economic hardship. Additionally, the Historical Center is now something of a depopulated architectural jewel whose "animation" must be brought in and sponsored by local shopowners and the Bahian state. Similar situations may be found in many UNESCO World Heritage Sites today but the Pelourinho, in light of Salvador's economic inequalities and ruling governmental coalition's of the 1990s, seems to have gone farther than most in sacrificing its population to the needs of tourist-based preservation.

Salvador has been the birthplace of many noted Brazilians, including musicians such as song-writer Dorival Caymmi, Música Popular Brasileira (MPB or *Brazilian Popular Music*) star Gal Costa, and

Grammy Award winner Gilberto Gil. Gil later went on to serve as a city council member (*vereador*) and is the Brazilian Minister of Culture in the cabinet of President Luiz Inácio Lula da Silva. Also internationally recognized are the city's Blocos Afros, such as Olodum, Ara Ketu, and Ilê Aiyê. Notable writers associated with Salvador include Jorge Amado, considered one of Brazil's greatest authors and fabulists, and João Ubaldo Ribeiro. The famous Brazilian visual artist Carybé is based in Salvador as well. Celebrities born in Salvador include supermodel Adriana Lima.

Climate

Salvador features a tropical rainforest climate with no discernable dry season. Temperatures are relatively constant throughout the course of the year, featuring warm and humid conditions. Salvador's driest month of the year is February, where the city receives on average 11 cm of precipitation. Salvador's wettest months are between May and July where 21 cm of rain falls during these 3 months.

Climate data for Salvador													
Month	Jan	Feb	Mar	Apr	May	Jun	Jul	Aug	Sep	Oct	Nov	Dec	Year
Record high °C (°F)	37 (99)	37 (99)	37 (99)	37 (99)	32 (90)	32 (90)	35 (95)	32 (90)	35 (95)	35 (95)	35 (95)	37 (99)	37 (99)
Average high °C (°F)	30 (86)	30 (86)	30 (86)	30 (86)	29 (84)	28 (82)	27 (81)	27 (81)	28 (82)	28 (82)	29 (84)	30 (86)	29 (84)
Daily mean °C (°F)	27 (81)	27 (81)	27 (81)	27 (81)	26 (79)	25 (77)	25 (77)	25 (77)	25 (77)	26 (79)	26 (79)	27 (81)	26 (79)
Average low °C (°F)	23 (73)	24 (75)	24 (75)	23 (73)	23 (73)	22 (72)	21 (70)	21 (70)	22 (72)	22 (72)	23 (73)	23 (73)	23 (73)
Record low °C (°F)	20 (68)	18 (64)	17 (63)	15 (59)	12 (54)	12 (54)	17 (63)	16 (61)	16 (61)	17 (63)	18 (64)	17 (63)	12 (54)
Precipitation cm (inches)	11 (4.3)	13 (5.1)	15 (5.9)	20 (7.9)	21 (8.3)	21 (8.3)	21 (8.3)	19 (7.5)	17 (6.7)	14 (5.5)	14 (5.5)	13 (5.1)	199 (78.3)
Source: Weatherbase													

Salvador, Bahia

Demographics

Main articles: Largest Cities of Northeast Region, Brazil and Demographics of Brazil

According to the IBGE of 2008, there were 3,716,000 people residing in the Metropolitan Region of Salvador. The population density was 4092.6 inhabitants per square kilometre (10600 /sq mi) (in the urban area). The last PNAD (National Research for Sample of Domiciles) census revealed the following numbers: 2,091,000 Brown (Multiracial) people (56.28%), 1,004,000 Black people (27.02%), 597,000 White people (16.06%), 12,000 Asian people (0.31%), 12,000 Amerindian people (0.31%).

Sunset in Plataforma Neighborhood.

With a current population estimated at 2,892,625 inhabitants, Salvador is the 3rd most populous city in Brazil, after São Paulo and Rio de Janeiro.

Most of the population is in part descended from Black African slaves, who were mainly Yoruba speakers from Nigeria, Ghana, Togo and Benin.

Population growth

Changing demographics of the city of Salvador

Source: Planet Barsa Ltda.

Religion

Religion	Percentage	Number
Catholic	60.54%	1,479,101
No religion	18.14%	443,236
Protestant	13.29%	324,785
Spiritist	2.53%	61,833
Umbandist	0.49%	11,959
Jewish	0.03%	698
Others	4.35%	106,320

Source: IBGE 2000.

Economy

Main articles: Economy of Salvador, Bahia and Economy of Brazil

Throughout Brazilian history Salvador has played an important role. In 1549 it became the first capital of Brazil. Throughout the colonial era Salvador was the colony's largest and most important city. Because of its strategic location on Brazil's northeastern coast, the city served as an important link in the Portuguese empire, maintaining close commercial ties with Portugal and Portuguese colonies in Africa and Asia. Salvador remained the preeminent city in Brazil until 1763 when it was replaced as the national capital by Rio de Janeiro. Salvador is a city that blends its rich historical past with a vibrant present. Recently constructed high-rise office and apartment buildings share the same block with colonial-era housing or commercial buildings. Modern hospitals are staffed by competent doctors and nursing staff, trained in the latest medical techniques. With its beaches, humid tropical climate, numerous up-to-date shopping malls and pleasant middle-class residential areas, the city has much to offer its residents. Economically Salvador is one of Brazil's more important cities. Since its founding the city has been one of Brazil's most prominent ports and international trading centers. Boasting a large oil refinery, a petrochemical plant and other important industries, the city has made great strides in reducing its historical dependence on agriculture for its prosperity.

Historic Centre in the morning.

Convent and Church of São Francisco in Historic Centre.

Salvador is the second most popular tourist destination in Brazil. Tourism and cultural activity are important generators of jobs and income, boosting the arts and the preservation of artistic and cultural heritage. Chief among the points of interest are its famous *Pelourinho* (named after the colonial pillories that once stood there) district, its historic churches, and its beaches. Salvador's tourism infrastructure is considered one of the most modern in Brazil, especially in terms of lodging. The city offers accommodation to suit all tastes and standards, from youth hostels to international hotels. Construction is one of the most important activities in the city, and many international (mainly from Spain, Portugal and England) and national developers are investing in the city and in the Bahian littoral zone.

Ford Motor Company has a plant in the Metropolitan Region of Salvador, in the city of Camaçari, assembling the Ford EcoSport, Ford Fiesta, Ford Fiesta Sedan. It is the only Automotive industry in

Northern and Northeastern Brazil. The industry employs 800 engineers.

In December 2001, Monsanto Company inaugurated, at the Petrochemical Pole of Camaçari, in Metropolitan Region of Salvador, the first plant of the company designed to produce raw materials for the herbicide Roundup in South America. The investment is equivalent to US$ 500 millions; US$ 350 millions were spent in this initial phase. The Camaçari Plant, the largest unit of Monsanto outside of the United States, is also the only Monsanto plant manufacturing raw materials for the Roundup production line. The company started the civil works for the new plant in January 2000.

The area of the unit is 631,000 square meters, including 200,000 square meters of constructed area. Upon completion of the two phases, it will employ 1,400 people, including direct (350) and indirect (1050) employments. With this plant in operation, Monsanto Company now contributes US$ 300 million to the Brazilian economy, avoiding the importation of US$ 150 million of raw materials.

The GDP for the city was R$ 24,072,400,000 (2006).

The per capita income for the city was R$ 8,870 (2006).

Economy	GDP (in reais)	GDP per capita (in reais)
2003	16,929,310,000	6,541
2004	19,887,968,000	7,557
2005	22,145,303,000	8,283
2006	24,072,400,000	8,870

Tourism and recreation

Main article: Tourism in Brazil

The Salvador coastline is one of the longest for cities in Brazil. There are 50 km (31 mi) of beaches distributed between the High City and the Low City, from Inema, in the railroad suburb to the Praia do Flamengo, on the other side of town. While the Low City beaches are bordered by the waters of the All Saints Bay (the country's most extensive bay), the High City beaches, from Farol da Barra to Flamengo, are bordered by the Atlantic Ocean. The exception is Porto da Barra Beach, the only High City beach located in the All Saints Bay.

The big hotels tend to be strung out along the orla (Atlantic seafront). There are also smaller hotels in Barra and Porto da Barra, others (generally less expensive) scattered along the principal thoroughfare of Avenida Sete de Setembro (shortened to "Avenida Sete" by the locals), and still others (usually inexpensive) in and around Pelourinho.

There are also pousadas (guest houses, or bed and breakfasts) in Barra, Pelourinho, and Santo Antônio (and other places as well, to be sure), and hostels (albergues) which are for the most part located in

Pelourinho (though a lot of the "pousadas" in Barra are hostels as well).

The capital's beaches range from calm inlets, ideal for swimming, sailing, diving and underwater fishing, as well as open sea inlets with strong waves, sought by surfers. There are also beaches surrounded by reefs, forming natural pools of stone, ideal for children.

Interesting places to visit near Salvador include:

- According to the British newspaper *The Guardian*, in 2007, Porto da Barra Beach was the 3rd best in the world.
- Salvador was selected the second destination by international tourists in Brazil, the city of Rio de Janeiro is the first.
- The large island of Itaparica in the Bay of All Saints - can be visited either by a car-ferry, or a smaller foot-passenger ferry which leaves from near the Mercado Modelo near the Lacerda Elevator.
- BA-099 Highway, or "Line of Coconut" and "Green Line" of towns and cities, with exquisite beaches, north of Salvador heading towards Sergipe state.
- Cachoeira in the *recôncavo* region - two hours by bus: a great centre of Candomblé with a pousada (inn) in the convent there.
- Morro de São Paulo in the Valença region across the Bay of All Saints – a lively island which can be reached by ferry from Salvador (1 hour), by plane, or by bus to Valença and then by 'Rapido' ('fast') speedboat or smaller ferry. Morro de São Paulo is formed by five villages of the Tinharé Island.

The city is served by many shopping malls: Shopping Iguatemi, Salvador Shopping, Shopping Barra, Shopping Paralela, Aeroclube Plaza Show, Shopping Piedade, Shopping Center Lapa, Shopping Itaigara, Caboatã Shopping, Casa Shopping Cidade, Out Let Center, Shopping Baixa Dos Sapateiros, Boulevard 161, Shopping Brotas Center, Shopping Do Pelô, Shopping Imbuí Plaza, Shopping Orixás Center, Shopping Sumaré.

Salvador has four parks, green areas protected, as Jardim dos Namorados Park, Costa Azul Park, Park of the City, Park of Pituaçu.

Jardim dos Namorados is located right next to Costa Azul Park and occupies an area of 15 hectares in Pituba, where many families used to spend their vacations in the 1950s. It was inaugurated in 1969, initially as a leisure area. It underwent a complete renovation in the 1990s, with the construction of an amphitheater with room for 500 people, sports courts, playgrounds and parking four cars and tourist buses.

Costa Azul Park occupies an area of approximately 55,000 square meters, and is located in the neighborhood that goes by the same name. It has football courts, gymnastics equipment, cycleways, jogging tracks, two playgrounds with an area for bicycles, sidewalks, restaurants, green areas, a parking lot with room for 150 vehicles and an amphitheater capable of receiving 600 people.

Park of the City is an important preservation area of the Atlantic forest. It was completely renovated in 2001, becoming a modern social, cultural and leisure place. The new park has 720 square meter of green area right in the middle of the city. Among the attractions are Praça das Flores (Flowers square), with more than five thousand ornamental plants and flowers. Besides its environment, the park has an infrastructure for children, with a special schedule of events taking place every October.

The park also has a medical station, special areas for encounters of students, tourists and senior citizens, a wide parking area with room for 270 vehicles, a 4,000 meter long jogging track, surrounding the entire park and an amphitheater with capacity for 600 people, where several cultural activities happen. Leisure and Gymnastics equipment can be found as well and the security is done by Florestal Police.

Created by state decree in 1973, Pituaçu Park occupies an area of 450 hectares and is one of the few Brazilian ecological parks located in an urban area. It is surrounded by Atlantic forest, with a good variety of plants and animals. There is also an artificial pond in the park, built in 1906 along with the Pituaçu Dam, whose purpose was to supply water to the city. There are a number of possible leisure activities, ranging from cycloboats rides on the pond, to an 18 km (11 mi) long cycloway circling the entire reserve. Completing this infrastructure there are several options for children to play, snack bars, ice cream parlors and restrooms. A museum is also located in the park. Espaço Cravo is an outdoor museum with 800 pieces created by Mario Cravo, comprising Totems, winged and three-dimensional figures, as well as drawings and paintings.

Education

Main article: Education in Brazil

Portuguese language is the official national language, and thus the primary language taught in schools. But English and Spanish are part of the official high school curriculum. There are also international schools, such as the Pan American School of Bahia. [2]

Educational institutions

The city has several universities:

- Universidade Federal da Bahia (UFBA) (Federal University of Bahia);
- Universidade Católica do Salvador (UCSal) (Catholic University of Salvador);
- Universidade do Estado da Bahia [3] (UNEB) (Bahia State University);
- Universidade Salvador [4] (UNIFACS) (Salvador University);
- Faculdade de Tecnologia e Ciências [5] (FTC) (College of Technology and Science);
- Centro Federal de Educação Tecnológica da Bahia [6] (Cefet-BA) (Federal Center of Technological Education of Bahia);
- Faculdade Ruy Barbosa [7] (FRB) (Ruy Barbosa College);

- Faculdade Castro Alves [8] (FCA) (Castro Alves College);
- Faculdade Jorge Amado [9] (FJA) (Jorge Amado College);
- Escola Bahiana de Medicina e Saúde Pública [10] (FBDC) (Bahiana College of Medicine and Public Health);
- and many others.

Portuguese schools

The city has several language schools of Portuguese for foreigners:

- Escola de Português [11]
- Fala-Brasil [12]
- Diálogo [13]
- Básica Língua [14]
- Sônia Portuguese [15]
- and others.

Primary and secondary schools

Top high schools of the city are Pan American School of Bahia, Anglo-Brasileiro Academy, Federal Institute of Bahia (IFBA - Cefet), Military College of Salvador, Anchieta Academy, Oficina Academy, Salesiano Academy, Miró Academy, Marista School of Salvador, Antônio Vieira Academy, Módulo Academy, Sartre Academy, São Paulo Academy, Cândido Portinari Academy, Integral Academy, São José Academy, Alfred Nobel Academy (now owned of the Sartre Academy), Nossa Senhora da Conceição Academy, Santíssimo Sacramento Academy, Diplomata Academy, Nossa Senhora do Resgate Academy, Gregor Mendel Academy and Thales de Azevedo State High School.

Historic Centre

Main article: Historic Centre (Salvador, Bahia)

Historic Centre of Salvador da Bahia*
UNESCO World Heritage Site

Old houses in the historical centre of Salvador.

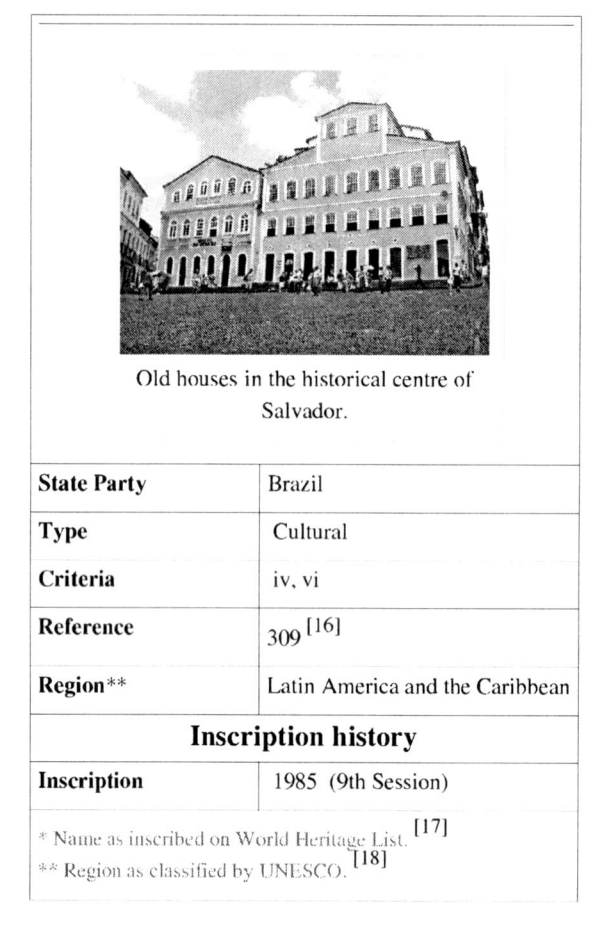

State Party	Brazil
Type	Cultural
Criteria	iv, vi
Reference	309 [16]
Region**	Latin America and the Caribbean

Inscription history

Inscription	1985 (9th Session)

* Name as inscribed on World Heritage List. [17]
** Region as classified by UNESCO. [18]

The Historic Centre of Salvador was designated in 1985 a World Heritage Site by UNESCO. The city represents a fine example the Portuguese urbanism from the middle of the 16th century with its higher administrative town and its lower commercial town, and a large portion of the city has retained the old character of its streets and colourful houses.

As the first capital of Portuguese America, Salvador cultivated slave labor and had its "pelourinhos" pillories installed in open places like the terreiro de Jesus and the squares know today as Thomé de Souza and Castro Alves. The "pelourinho" was a symbol of authority and justice, for some, and lashings and injustice for the majority. The one erected for a short time in what is now the Historical Center, and later moved to what is now the Praça da Piedade (Square of Piety), ended up lending its name to the historical and architectural complex of Pelourinho, part of the city's historical center.

Since 1992, the Pelourinho neighborhood has been subject to a nearly US$ 100 million "restoration" that has led to the rebuilding of hundreds of buildings' facades and the expulsion of the vast majority of the neighborhood's Afro-descendent population. This process has given rise to substantial political debate in the State of Bahia, since the Pelourinho's former residents have been for the most part excluded from the renovation's economic benefits (reaped by a few). A major restoration effort resulted in making the area a highly desirable tourist attraction.

Salvador's considerable wealth and status during colonial times (as capital of the colony during 250 years and which gave rise to the Pelourinho) is reflected in the magnificence of its colonial palaces, churches and convents, most of them dating from the 17th and 18th centuries. These include:

- Cathedral of Salvador: Former Jesuit church of the city, built in the second half of the 17th century. Fine example of Mannerist architecture and decoration.
- Convent and Church of São Francisco: Franciscan convent and church dating from the first half of the 18th century is another fine example of the Portuguese colonial architecture. The Baroque decoration of the church is among the finest in Brazil.
- Church of Nosso Senhor do Bonfim: Rococo church with Neoclassical inner decoration.

The image of Nosso Senhor do Bonfim is the most venerated in the city, and the Feast of Our Lord of Good Ending (*Festa de Nosso Senhor do Bonfim*) in January is the most important in the city after Carnival.

- Mercado Modelo (Model Market): In 1861, at the Cayrú Square, the Customs Building was constructed, with a rotunda (large circular room with a domed ceiling) at the back end, where ships anchored to unload their merchandise. In 1971, a market began to operate in the Customs Building, and thirteen years later, it caught fire, burned down, and underwent reform. Today, there are 200 stands with a variety of arts and crafts made in Bahia as well as other states in northeastern region of Brazil, two restaurants, and several bars that serve typical drinks and appetizers.

Historic Centre of Salvador.

- Elevador Lacerda (Lacerda Elevator): Inaugurated in 1873, this elevator was planned and built by the businessman Antônio Francisco de Lacerda, The four elevator cages connect the 72 metres (236 ft) between the Thomé de Souza Square in the upper city, and the Cayru Square in the lower city. In each run, which lasts for 22 seconds, the elevator transports 128 persons, 24 hours a day.

Culture

Salvador's historical and cultural aspects were inherited by the miscigenation of such ethnic groups as Native-Indian, African, and European. This mixture can be seen in the religion, golden cuisine, cultural manifestations, and custom of Bahia's people.

Literature

Main article: Literature of Brazil

As the capital of colonial Brazil until 1763, Salvador was an important cultural centre since the 16th century, as reflected in the large number of prominent literary figures associated with colonial Salvador, usually educated in the religious schools of the convents of the city and in the University of Coimbra in Portugal. *Frei Vicente do Salvador* (1564–1635), a Bahia-born Franciscan friar who studied in the Jesuit School of Salvador, was the author of the first book on Brazilian history written by a Brazil-born author.

Fort of São Diogo.

Gregório de Mattos, born in Salvador in 1636, was also educated by the Jesuits. He became the most important Baroque poet in colonial Brazil for his religious and satirical works. Father António Vieira was born in Lisbon in 1608, but was raised and educated in the Jesuit school of Salvador and died in the city in 1697. His erudite sermons have earned him the title of best writer of the Portuguese language in the Baroque era.

After the Independence of Brazil (1822), Salvador continued to play an important role in Brazilian literature. Significant 19th century writers associated with the city include Romantic poet Castro Alves (1847–1871) and diplomat Ruy Barbosa (1849–1923). In the 20th century, Bahia-born Jorge Amado (1912–2001), although not born in Salvador, helped popularize the culture of the city around the world in novels such as *Jubiabá*, *Dona Flor e Seus Dois Maridos*, and *Tenda dos Milagres*, the settings of which are in Salvador.

Isometric view of the Salvador Bahia Pelourinho's Anchieta Plaza, cut from a Laser Scan.

Religion

Main article: Religion in Brazil

In Salvador, religion is a major contact point between Portuguese and African influences and, more recently, Brazil's version of a North American-influenced Pentecostalism. Salvador was the seat of the first bishopric in colonial Brazil (established 1551), and the first bishop, *Pero Fernandes Sardinha*, arrived already in 1552. The Jesuits, led by the Manuel da Nóbrega, also arrived in the 16th century and worked in converting the Indigenous peoples of the region to Roman Catholicism.

Many religious orders came to the city, following its foundation: Franciscans, Benedictines and Carmelites. Subsequently to them are created the Third Orders, the Brotherhoods, and Fraternities, which were composed mainly of professional and social groups. The most prominent of these orders were the Terceira do Carmo Order and the de São Francisco Order, founded by white men, and the Nossa Senhora do Rosário and São Beneditino Brotherhoods, composed of black men. In many churches maintained by religious men, were housed the Santíssimo Sacramento brotherhoods.

Besides these organizations, the expansion of Catholicism in the city was consolidated through social care work. Santa Casa the Misericórdia was one oh the institution that did this kind of work, maintaining hospitals, shelters for the poor and the elderly, as well providing assistance to convicts and to those who would face death penalties. The convents, on their part, were cultural and religious formation centers, offering seminar coursed that often were attende by the lay.

Even with the present evolution, and the growth of Protestantism and other religions in the city, the Catholic faith remains as one of its most distinctive features, drawing a lot of people to its hundreds of churches. Some aspects, like the use of Portuguese in the Masses, the simplification of the liturgy, and the adoption of "pop" religious songs are key factors to the triumph of Catholicism. In the Nossa Senhora do Rosário dos Pretos Church, Masses are held in the Yorubá language, making use of African chants and typical clothes, which attract many people from the black communities.

Protestant Church in Iguatemi Neighborhood.

Most enslaved Africans in Bahia were brought from Sub-Saharan Africa, especially the Yoruba-speaking nation (*Iorubá* or *Nagô* in Portuguese) from present-day Nigeria. The enslaved were forced to convert to Roman Catholicism, but their original religion, Candomblé, has survived in spite of prohibitions and persecutions. The enslaved Africans managed to preserve their religion by attributing the names and characteristics of their Candomblé deities to Catholic saints with similar qualities.

Hence, as former pagan Christians once associated Pagan deities with the saints, enslaved Africans in Bahia transformed their faiths into a syncretic form of religion that still attempts to please both their own roots and the faith imposed by their masters and those caught in between both traditions. Thus, up to today, even nominal Catholics take part in Candomblé rituals in the *terreiros* or "centros". Candomblé is based on the cult of the Orishas (*Orixás*), like Obatala (*Oxalá*), father of humankind; Ogoun (*Ogum*), god of the war and iron; Yemanja (*Iemanjá*), goddess of the sea, rivers and lakes.

These religious entities have been syncretised with some Catholic entities. For instance, Salvador's Feast of Bonfim, celebrated in January, is dedicated to both Our Lord of Bonfim (Jesus Christ) and Oxalá. Another important feast is the Feast de Yemanja every February 2, on the shores of the borough of Rio Vermelho in Salvador, on the day the church celebrates Our Lady of the Navigators. December 8, Immaculate Conception Day for Catholics, is also commonly dedicated to Yemanja' with votive offerings made in the sea throughout the Brazilian coast.

Religious syncretism is defined as the combination of two or more creeds. In Brazil, especially in Bahia, it came up as a solution for the slaves who were prohibited of practicing their religion, so they pretended to be worshiping catholic saints while in reality they were venerating their own deities. Hence, associating an orixá (Candoblé deity) to a catholic was a strategy used by black people to maintain their beliefs and rituals alive, while they fooled their masters, making them believe that their devotion was to the catholic saints.

The lives of catholic saints and their own physical features, portrayed on sculptures and drawings, made the identification with the orixás easier. Salvador is a city where different ethnic and cultural aspects are mixed up, but religious syncretism remains as one of its most intriguing features. Its ancient churches are a proof of the power of Catholicism, which was brought by the Portuguese and forced upon Blacks and Indigenous.

Cuisine

Main article: Cuisine of Brazil

Local cuisine of Salvador.

The local cuisine, spicy and based on seafood (shrimp, fish), strongly relies on typically African ingredients and techniques, and is much appreciated throughout Brazil and internationally. The most typical ingredient is *azeite-de-dendê*, an oil extracted from a palm tree (*Elaeis guineensis*) brought from West Africa to Brazil during colonial times.

Using the milky coconut juice, they prepared a variety of sea-food based dishes, such as Ensopados, Moquecas and

Escabeche. The sugar cane bagasse was mixed with molasses and Rapadura, in the creation of coconut desserts like Cocada Branca and Preta. The remaining of the Portuguese Stew sauce was mixed with manioc flour to make a mush, which is a traditional Indian dish. In the markets of Salvador, it is possible to find stands selling typical dishes of the colonial era. In the Sete Portas Market, customers eat Mocotó on Friday nights since the 1940s, when the market was inaugurated. In the restaurants of Mercado Modelo (Model Market), Sarapatel, stews and several fried dishes are served regularly. In the São Joaquim, Santa Bárbara and São Miguel markets, there are stands selling typical food. They are also sold at stands located on the beaches, specially crab stews and oysters. The restaurants that sell typical dishes are located mostly along the coast and in Pelourinho. They prepare a wide variety of recipes that take palm tree oil.

Traditional dishes include *caruru*, *vatapá*, *acarajé*, *bobó-de-camarão*, *moqueca* baiana, and *abará*. Some of these dishes, like the acarajé and abará, are also used as offerings in Candomblé rituals. An acarajé is basically a deep-fried "bread" made from mashed beans from which the skins have been removed (reputedly feijão fradinho "black-eyed peas" but in reality almost always the less expensive brown beans so ubiquitous in Bahia). But Salvador is not only typical food. Other recipes created by the slaves were the Haussá Rice (rice and jerked beef cooked together), the Munguzá, used as offering to the Candomblé deity Oxalá (who is the father of all deities, according to the religion) pleased the matrons very much. So did the Bolinhos the Fubá, the Cuscuz (cornmeal) and the Mingau (porridge). According to Arany Santana, the Ipetê (used in the rituals to the deity Oxum) became the Shrimp Bobó (a kind of mush), and the Akará (honoring the deities Xangô and Iansã) became the world-famous Acarajé. Who comes here also has a large number of restaurants specialized on international cuisine. There also places that serve dishes from other states of Brazil, especially from Minas Gerais and the Northeast region.

Capoeira

Capoeira is a unique mix of dance and martial art of Afro-Brazilian origin, combining agile dance moves with unarmed combat techniques. Capoeira in Portuguese literally means "chicken coop." The presence of capoeira in Brazil is directly connected to the importation of African slaves by the Portuguese, and Salvador is considered the centre of origin of the modern capoeira branches. The initial purpose of Capoeira's emergence was to boost the slaves morale, remind them of their homeland through music and to defend themselves against aggression from their owners. The art of Capoeira is uniquely identified by

Capoeira in Salvador.

swinging hips, arm stands, head butts and sweeping feet movements. The art required a good level of agility and core strength. In the first half of the 20th century, Salvador-born masters Mestre Bimba and

Mestre Pastinha founded capoeira schools and helped standartise and popularise the art in Brazil and the world. The practice of Capoeira was banned in 1892, though in 1937 it was made legal.

Capoeira practices are accompanied by special music and songs. Musical instruments used in capoeira music include the berimbau, atabaque, pandeiro, agogô, and caxixi. Capoeira has moved from the senzalas and quilombos of Brazil to New York, Berlin, Australia, and just about every place in between.

Museums

Salvador Historical Centre.

The artistic, cultural and social heritage of Salvador is preserved in museums. From Museu de Arte da Bahia (MAB), which is the oldest in the State, to Museu Náutico, the newest, the first capital of Brazil preserve unique pieces of history. Every museum in the sate is an unusual journey. The collection have such an immense symbolical value that no financial figure could ever measure.

Even so, the importance of Salvador's museums has drawn the interest of experts from Brazil and abroad. There we can find valuable pieces of religious art, ornamental items from the old manors and also objects that belonged to the old families and public figures of the state. The Arte Sacra and Abelardo Rodrigues museums are must, see programs. They both have the biggest sacra art collection in the country. Another obligatory tour is to Museu de Arte da Bahia.

Museu de Arte da Bahia has paintings, Chinese porcelain, furniture and sacra images from the 17th and 18th centuries. Museu Costa Pinto has private, owned items such as, pieces of art, crystal objects, furniture from the 18th and 19th centuries, tapestry, sacra pieces and Chinese porcelain. The golden jewelry and the 27 ornamental silver buckles are the most precious in the entire collection.

Another important museum is Museu da Cidade, where many items that help to preserve the heritage of old Salvador are kept. There we can find thematic objects that belonged to public personalities in the state like dolls, orixá statues and religious images. There is also an art gallery located inside of the museums. There is also Fundação Casa de Jorge Amado, with pictures, objects and the life's stories of the author of memorable novels that portray old Bahia like, Gabriela – Cravo e Canela, Dona Flor e Seus Dois Maridos, O País do Carnaval and Tieta do Agreste.

Some churches and monasteries also have museums located in their premises. Examples of this are the Carmo da Misericórdia and São Bento Museums. After the renovation of the Forts, were created Museu Náutico, in Forte de Santo Antonio da Barra (Farol da Barra) and Museu da Comunicação, in Forte São Diogo. Other important museums that are scattered through Salvador are: Museu do Cacau, Museu geológico do Estado, Museu tempostal, Solar do Ferrão, Museu de Arte Antiga e Popular Henriqueta M

Catharino, Museu Eugênio Teixeira Leal and Museu das Portas do Carmo.

Carnival/Carnaval

Main articles: Bahian Carnival and Brazilian Carnival

According to the Guinness Book of Records, the carnival or *Carnaval* of Salvador da Bahia is the biggest street party on the planet. For an entire week, almost 2 million people celebrate throughout 25 kilometers (15 miles) of streets, avenues and squares. The direct organization of the party involves the participation of 100 thousand people. Its dimensions are gigantic. Salvador receives an average of 800 thousand visitors from municipalities located as far as 150 kilometers (93 miles) away, from several States of Brazil and from a number of other countries (Europe, U.S.A., Israel, Argentina, Australia, and many others).

The cover was done by 2,446 professionals in local press, national, and international. The carnival was broadcast to 135 countries through 65 radio stations, 75 magazines, 139 producers of video, 97 newspapers (21 international), 14 tv stations, and 168 websites.

Salvador's Street Carnival is the biggest in the world.

Rei Momo: The King of Carnival, Momo, is handed the keys to the city in the morning, on the Thursday before Fat Tuesday, and the party officially begins. Camarotes: These grandstands line the street in the neighborhood of Campo Grande. Watch the show from here without being trampled by the crowd. Trios Eléctricos: Outfitted with deafening sound systems, these 60-foot-long trucks carry a kick line of gyrating, scantily clad dancers along with the city's best-loved performers, among them Ivete Sangalo, Daniela Mercury, Cláudia Leitte, Chiclete com Banana, Carlinhos Brown, and others.

The music played during Carnaval includes Axé and Samba-reggae. Many "blocos" participate in Carnaval, the "blocos afros" like Malé Debalé, Olodum and Filhos de Gandhi being the most famous of them. Carnival is heavily policed. Stands with five or six seated police officers are erected everywhere and the streets are constantly patrolled by police groups moving in single file.

The Osmar Circuit: goes from Campo Grande to Castro Alves square, The Downtown Circuit, in Downtown and Pelourinho, and The Dodô Circuit: goes from Farol da Barra to Ondina, along the coast. The Osmar circuit is the oldest circuit. It is also where the event's most traditional groups parades. In Dodô, where the artist box seats are located, the party becomes lively toward the end of the afternoon and it continues until morning.

The three Carnival Circuits are:

- The Campo Grande - Praça Castro Alves Circuit, also called the "Osmar" Circuit, or simply the "Avenidas" ("Avenues");
- The Barra - Ondina Circuit, also called the "Dodô" Circuit;
- The Pelourinho Circuit, also called the "Batatinha" ("Little potato") Circuit.

Summer Festival

The Salvador Summer Festival, is an annual five-day music extravaganza that this year is to feature its usual who's who of Brazilian popular music: Daniela Mercury, Eva, Capital Inicial, Titãs, Skank, Jota Quest, Ivete Sangalo, Chiclete com Banana, Ana Carolina, and others. The price of admission has yet to be set. Attractions international as Akon, Gloria Gaynor, Men at Work, Eagle-Eye Cherry, Fatboy Slim, Ben Harper, Manu Chao, West Life, The Gladiators and Alanis Morissette already sang in Summer Festival.

Funk and Bahia Funk Dances

Main article: Music of Brazil

Funk has become a musical genre in Brazil that exemplifies how many influences, in and out of Brazil, merged with Brazilian culture in the 20th century to form a new hybrid sound. Funk originated as a black American form of music that started in the 1960s and included artists like James Brown and The Funk Brothers.

Amphitheater of City Park of Salvador.

Although funk was embraced by many parts of Brazil, its sound would eventually become localized so the music would differ from city to city. This difference can be viewed with the funk scenes in Rio de Janeiro and Salvador. The music and the environment are all representative of the city where one listens to funk music.

For instance, the music played in Salvador at a Black Bahia Funk Ball is more American than its counterpart in Rio de Janeiro. Music material from Rio, which sells reasonably well around Rio, is poorly known in Salvador and, in any case, held to be inferior and "less modern" than funk sung in English. Another difference can be seen with the funk dancehalls. The Ball incorporates the entire setting, which entails the attire, the slang, the specific way of dancing break, the decoration, the organization of permanent dance groups. These dancehalls are a place for everyone to come together to have fun before the start of another work week. Even the dance rivalries are not true rivalries in the sense that the dance groups do not physically fight one another. The group members do all their battling on the dance floor, using their dance moves as their weapons to demonstrate their dance skill and superiority.

Theatre

The theatres of the city are: Castro Alves Theatre (TCA), Sala do Côro (mini Theatre in Castro Alves Theatre), IRDEB Theatre (TV Educativa), SENAC Theatre (Pelourinho), ICÉIA Theatre, Museu Eugênio Teixeira Leal Theatre (Pelourinho), Barra Theatre, Espaço Xisto Theatre, Maria Betânia Theatre, Jorge Amado Theatre, Diplomata Theatre, Sesi Rio Vermelho Theatre, Vila Velha Theatre, XVIII Theatre, ISBA Theatre, Santo Antônio Theatre, ACBEU Theatre, Anchieta Theatre, Nazaré Theatre, ICBA Theatre, Gamboa Theatre, Gregório de Mattos Theatre, Módulo Theatre, Miguel Santana Theatre, Cultural Theatre, Cine Casa do Comércio Theatre, Dias Gomes Theatre (Sindicato dos Comerciários), Plataforma Theatre.

Libraries

The first books that arrived in Salvador, were brought by the Jesuits, who came with Tomé de Souza. The first libraries or bookstores that appeared were under the control of the religious missionaries and were mostly composed of books on religion. Areas combining leisure and culture, Salvador's libraries are an entertainment option for tourists and researchers. Some of these spaces have religious origins, some of them are temples of knowledge accessible only to a few, due to the fragility of the relics they contain.

The Benedictine, Carmelites, Franciscans and Capuchin orders have in Salvador, titles related to fundamental aspects of the state's history, being important for a comprehensive view of the political, religious, moral and artistic formation of the city. Conversely to the restrictive religious libraries, the public libraries and the ones linked to institutions that give incentive to culture and information, provide the general public with a variety of titles. Salvador's libraries are: Arquivo Histórico Municipal, Biblioteca Acbeu, Biblioteca Aloísio da França Rocha, Biblioteca Anísio Teixeira, Biblioteca da Fundação João Fernandes da Cunha, Biblioteca do Centro Cultural Prof. Ademar Cardoso, Biblioteca do Museu de Arte da Bahia, Biblioteca do Serviço Social do Comércio, Biblioteca Juracy Magalhães Júnior, Biblioteca Ministro Coqueijo Costa, Biblioteca Monteiro Lobato, Biblioteca Mosteiro de São Bento da Bahia, Biblioteca Pública do Estado da Bahia, Centro de Documentação Cultural sobre a Bahia, Gabinete Português de Leitura.

Handcraft

Main article: Brazilian art

The handcraft legacy of Bahia using only raw materials (straw, leather, clay, wood, seashells and beads), the most rudimentary crafts are reasonably inexpensive. Other pieces are created with the use of metals like gold, silver, copper and brass. The most sophisticated ones are ornamented with precious and semi-precious gems. The craftsmen and women generally choose religion as the main theme of their work.

They portray the images of Catholic saints and Candomble deities on their pieces. The good luck charms such as the clenched fist, the four-leaf clover, the garlic and the famous Bonfim ribbons express the city's religious syncretism. Nature is also portrayed on these pieces, reflecting the local wildlife. Music appears in the atabaque drums, the rain sticks, the water drums and the famous berimbau, along with other typical instruments.

Salvador holds an international reputation as a city where musical instruments that produce unique sounds are made. These instruments are frequently used by world-famous artists in their recording sessions. A place to see Salvador's handcrafts production is Mercado Modelo, which is the biggest handcraft center in Latin America. Pieces can also be purchased at Instituto de Artesanato de Mauá and at Instituto do Patrimônio Artístico e Cultural (IPAC). These are organizations that promote typical art in Bahia. In Pelourinho there are a variety of stores selling souvenirs to visitors.

Human rights and LGBT rights

Main articles: Human rights in Brazil and LGBT rights in Brazil

Salvador is also home to the oldest, continuous gay rights and human rights organization in Brazil, the Grupo Gay da Bahia (GGB), which organizes weekly gatherings in the old quarter Pelourinho (Historic Centre of Salvador). Established by Dr. Luiz Mott in 1980 and currently headed by Marcelo Cerqueira, GGB has played a central role in the lesbian, gay, bisexual and transgender equality movement both in Bahia and across Brazil, and has helped to educate the local population on HIV and AIDS prevention and human rights abuses. Today, the city has one of the lowest numbers of HIV infections per capita in Brazil.

Salvador's gay pride parade is now one of the largest in Brazil, approximately 800,000 people in 2010. The Public Defender of the State of Bahia, located in many cities of the state, including Salvador, fights the discrimination on account of the race, color, sexual orientation, and religious orientation, for example.

The city offers many options: gay night clubs (San Sebastian Salvador, Off Club, and many others); gay saunas (Sauna Paradise, Esgrima, Sauna Rio's, Sauna Campos, Sauna Olympus, Sauna Phoenix and Thermas Persona); gay bars (Beco da Off, Beco dos Artistas, Babalotin, and many others); gay beaches (Porto da Barra Beach - right part and Artistas Beach). The annual LGBT event Hell & Heaven, in

Costa do Sauípe, is one of the largest LGBT events in Brazil.

Transportation

International Airport

Deputado Luís Eduardo Magalhães International Airport is located in an area of more than 6 million square meters between sand dunes and native vegetation. The airport lies 20 km (12 mi) north of Downtown Salvador and the road to the airport has already become one of the city's main scenic attractions. In 2007, the airport handled 5,920,573 passengers and 91,043 aircraft movements, placing it 5th busiest airport in Brazil in terms of passengers. The airport's use has been growing at an average of 14% a year and now is responsible for more than 30% of passenger movement in Northeastern Brazil. Nearly 35 thousand people circulate daily through the passenger terminal. The airport generates more than 16 thousand direct and indirect jobs, to serve a daily average of over 10 thousand passengers, 250 takeoffs and landings of 100 domestic and 16 international flights. Buses between the city centre and the airport are fairly frequent and cheaper than taxis. Buses also go to Rodoviária (Bus Terminal), which is the city's main bus station and located 5 km (3.1 mi) from the city centre.

There are good cafes and fast food restaurants at the airport. A bar offers alcoholic or soft drinks. There are several shops in the terminal building selling a variety of items, including fashion clothing, jewellery, gift items and books and magazines. There is also a pharmacy in the terminal building. Buses between the city centre and the airport are fairly frequent. Take the Praça da Sé (Sé Square)/Aeroporto bus. It is much cheaper than going by taxi. Buses also go to Rodoviária (Bus Terminal), which is the city's main bus station and located 5 km (3.1 mi) from the city centre. The car park of the airport, is located near the terminal building and has parking spaces for 600 cars. In addition to domestic and regional services, the airport has non-stop flights to Miami, United States, Madrid, Spain, Frankfurt, Germany, Lisbon, Portugal, London, United Kingdom, Montevideo, Uruguay, Santiago, Chile, Buenos Aires, Argentina, and Asunción, Paraguay. Its IATA airport code is SSA and the first in Northeastern Brazil.

Port

Main article: Port of Salvador

With cargo volume that grows year after year following the same economic development rhythm implemented in the State, the Port of Salvador, located in the Bahia de Todos os Santos, holds status as the port with the highest movement of containers of the North/Northeast and the second-leading fruit exporter in Brazil. The port's facilities operate from 8:00 AM to 12:00 PM and from 1:30 PM to 5:30 PM.

The ability to handle high shipping volume has positioned the port of Salvador for new investments in technological modernization, and the port is noted for implementing a high level of operational flexibility and competitive rates. The goal of port officials is to offer the necessary infrastructure for the movement of goods, while simultaneously meeting the needs of international importers and exporters.

Metro

Main article: Salvador Metro

Salvador Metro System is under construction, and its 1st phase will be ready in March 2008, between Lapa and Acceso Norte Stations, and in 2009 will be ready the stations between Acceso Norte and Pirajá. In 2009 it will have 12.5 km (7.8 mi) and 8 stations and will have link with the bus system. The citizen could take a bus to the metro station and there take the train without paying again. A contract for the supply and installation of systems and rolling stock for the first metro line in Salvador, was signed on July 24 with Metro Salvador. Salvador Metro also has a 25-year operating and maintenance concession, renewable for a further 25 years. The metro will be Brazil's eighth.

The main shareholders in Metro Salvador are the Spanish companies Construcciones y Auxiliar de Ferrocarriles, Dimetronic, and ICF. It is expected that Metro Salvador will invest US$ 150 million in rolling stock and signalling and telecommunications equipment. The contract covers the first 11.9 km (7.4 mi) line from Pirajá to Lapa, which is due to open in 2003. The project is also financed by a US$ 150 million World Bank loan and contributions from the federal, Bahia state, and Salvador city governments.

Highways

The BR-101 and BR-116 federal highways cross Bahia from north to south, connecting Salvador to the rest of the country. At the Feira de Santana junction, take the BR-324 state highway. The capital of Bahia is served by several coach companies from almost every Brazilian state. BR-242, starting at São Roque do Paraguaçu (transversal direction), is linked to BR-116, bound to the middle–west region. Among the state highways stands BA-099, which makes connection to the north coast and BA-001, which makes connection to the south of Bahia. Buses provide direct service to most major Brazilian cities, including Rio de Janeiro, São Paulo, and Brasília, as well as regional destinations. In 2007, the city had 586,951 vehicles, the largest number of the Northern and Northeastern Brazil.

Green Line Highway.

Four paved highways connect the city to the national highway system. Running north from the Farol (lighthouse) de Itapoã are hundreds of miles of wonderful beaches. These beaches are accessible via the BA-099 Highway or (Line of Coconut and Green Line), a (toll) road, kept in excellent condition, running parallel to the coast, with access roads leading off to the coast itself. The road runs along dunes of snow-white sand, and the coast itself is an almost unbroken line of coconut palms. The communities along this coast range from fishing villages to Praia do Forte.

Distances

- Aracaju: 356 km (221 mi);
- Maceió: 632 km (393 mi);
- Recife: 839 km (521 mi);
- João Pessoa: 949 km (590 mi);
- Natal: 1126 km (700 mi);
- Fortaleza: 1389 km (863 mi);
- Belo Horizonte: 1430 km (890 mi);
- Brasília: 1540 km (960 mi);
- Rio de Janeiro: 1730 km (1070 mi);
- São Paulo: 1960 km (1220 mi);
- Curitiba: 2385 km (1482 mi);
- Florianópolis: 2682 km (1667 mi);
- Porto Alegre: 3090 km (1920 mi).

2nd Naval district of Brazilian Navy.

Neighborhoods

Although the creation of Salvador was masterminded by the Kingdom of Portugal and its project conducted by the Portuguese engineer Luís Dias (who was responsible for the city's original design), the continuous growth of the capital through the decades was completely spontaneous. The walls of the city-fortress could not hold the expansion of the city, towards the Carmo and the area where now stands Castro Alves Square. At the time of its foundation, Salvador had only two squares and the first neighborhood ever built here was the Historic City Center. Pelourinho and Carmo came subsequently, created as a consequence of the growing need of space that the religious orders had. With the rapid expansion, the neighborhoods grew and many of them were clustered in the same area, so today there aren't accurate records as to their exact number. For urban management purposes, the city is currently divided on 17 political-administrative zones. However, due to their very cultural relevance and to postal conveniences, the importance of the neighborhoods of Salvador remains intact. They represent the city's lively atmosphere and its cosmopolitan character.

Salvador is divided into a number of distinct neighborhoods, with the most well known districts being Pelourinho, the Historic Centre, Comércio, and Downtown, all located in West Zone. Barra, with its Farol da Barra, beaches and which is where one of the Carnival circuits begins, Barra is home of the Portuguese Hospital and Spanish Hospital, the neighborhood is located in South Zone. Vitória, a neighborhood with many high rise buildings, is located in South Zone. Campo Grande, with its Dois de Julho Square and the monument to Bahia's independence, is also located in South Zone, as is Graça, an important residential area.

Salvador Skyline.

Ondina, with Salvador's Zoobotanical Garden and the site where the Barra-Ondina Carnival circuit ends, the neighborhood is home of the Spanish Club, is also a neighborhood in the South Zone.

Itaigara, Pituba, Horto Florestal, Caminho das Árvores, Loteamento Aquárius, Brotas, Stiep, Costa Azul, Armação, Jaguaribe and Stella Maris are the wealthiest neighborhoods in the East Zone and the city. Rio Vermelho, a neighborhood with a rich architectural history and numerous restaurants and bars, is located in the South Zone. Itapoã, known throughout Brazil as the home of Vinicius de Moraes and for being the setting of the song "Tarde em Itapoã", is located in East Zone.

The Northwest area of the city in along the Bay of All Saints, also known as *Cidade Baixa* ("Lower city"), contains the impoverished suburban neighborhoods of Periperi, Paripe, Lobato, Liberdade, Nova Esperança, and Calçada. The neighborhood of Liberdade (Liberty) has the largest proportion of Afro-Brazilians of Salvador and Brazil.

Sports

Main articles: 2014 FIFA World Cup and Sports in Brazil

Salvador provides visitors and residents with various sport activities. The Fonte Nova Stadium, also known as Estádio Octávio Mangabeira is a football stadium inaugurated on January 28, 1951 in Salvador, Bahia, with a maximum capacity of 66,080 people. The stadium is owned by the Bahia government, and is the home ground of Esporte Clube Bahia. Its formal name honors Octávio Cavalcanti Mangabeira, a civil engineer, journalist, and former Bahia state governor from 1947 to 1954. The stadium is nicknamed Fonte Nova, because it is located at Ladeira das Fontes das Pedras. Esporte Clube Bahia and Esporte Clube Vitória are Salvador's main football teams. Esporte Clube Bahia has won 2 national titles, Brazil's Cup in 1959 and the Brazilian League in 1988, while Esporte Clube Vitória was a runner up in the Brazilian league in 1993. The stadium was recently closed due to an aciddent, and the matchs now happen in another stadium, in Pituaçu.

Salvador has two large green areas for the practice of golf. Cajazeiras Golf and Country Club has a 18-hole course, instructors, caddies and equipment for rent. Itapuã Golf club, located in the area of the

Sofitel Hotel, has a 9-hole course, equipment store, caddies and clubs for rent. Tennis is very popular among Salvador's elites, with a great number of players and tournaments in the city's private clubs. Brasil Open, the country's most important tournament happens every year in Bahia.

Skate in Jardim dos Namorados Park.

During the last decades, volleyball has grown steadily in Salvador, especially after the gold medal won by Brazil in the 1992 Summer Olympics in Barcelona. The most important tournaments in Bahia are the State Championship, the State League tournament and the Primavera Games, and the main teams are Associação Atlética da Bahia, Bahiano de Tênis, and Clube the Regatas Itapagipe. There are also beach volleyball events. Salvador has housed many international tournaments. Federação Bahina de Voleibol (the state league) can inform the schedule of tournaments. Bowling is practiced both by teenagers and adults in Salvador. Boliche do Aeroclube and Space Bowling are equipped with automatic lanes as well as a complete bar infrastructure.

Bahia's basketball league exists since 1993 and has 57 teams. The sport is very popular in the city of Salvador, especially among students. There are several courts scattered across the city, where is possible to play for free, like the one located at Bahia Sol square, where people with spinal cord lesions play. There are also several gymnasiums, in clubs like Bahiano de Tênis and Associação Atlética and the Antonio Balbino Gymnasiums (popularly known as "Balbininho"), which is an arena that can hold up to 7,000 people.

Todos os Santos Bay and Salvador's climatic conditions are ideal for competition and recreational sailing. The city is equipped with good infrastructure for practice of sailing, such as rental and sale of dock space, boat maintenance, restaurants, snack bar, convenience stores, nautical products stores, boat rental agencies, VHF and SSB communication systems, events, and total assistance to crews. The large number of sailing events organized by clubs and syndicates, like oceanic races and typical boats (wooden fishing boats and canoes) races, demonstrates the sport's growing force. Currently, Salvador has a national racing schedule with dozens of events, also receiving the Mini Transat 6.50 and Les Illes du Soleil races.

Rowing boat races started in the city more than a hundred years ago. It was originally practiced by young men from traditional families, who spent their summer vacations there. The sport is a leisure option in Cidade Baixa (the lower part of the city). Esporte Clube Vitória and Clube São Salvador were the pioneers in the sport. Nowadays, these two entities and also Clube de Regatas Itapagipe lead the competitions that take place in the city. With the recent renovation of the Dique do Tororó area, Salvador received new lanes for the practice of the sport.

Human development

The human development of Salvador varies greatly by locality, reflecting the spatial segregation and vast socioeconomic inequalities in the city. In 2000, there are neighborhoods with very high human development indexes equal to or greater than the indexes of some Scandinavian countries, but also those in the lower range in line with, for example, North Africa.

Neighborhoods and localities champions:

- Itaigara (0.971) - *(Greater than Iceland, Norway - 0.968)*
- Caminho das Árvores - Iguatemi (0.968) - *(Equal to Iceland, Norway - 0.968)*
- Caminho das Árvores/Pituba - Loteamento Aquárius (0.968) - *(Equal to Iceland, Norway - 0.968)*
- Brotas or Santiago de Compostela (0.968) - *(Equal to Iceland, Norway - 0.968)*
- Pituba - Paulo VI Avenue, Nossa Senhora da Luz Park (0.965) - *(Greater than Australia - 0.962)*

Neighborhoods and localities in last place:

- Rural Zone/Areia Branca, CIA Airport-Ceasa (0.652) - *(Greater than Namibia - 0.650)*
- Coutos/Fazenda Coutos, Felicidade (0.659) - *(less than Vanuatu (0.670) and Guatemala - 0.673)*
- Paz Neighborhood/Itapuã - Exposições Park (0.664) - *(less than Vanuatu (0.670) and Guatemala - 0.673)*

Notable residents

- Acelino Freitas, boxer.
- Antônio Carlos Magalhães, politician.
- Antônio Carlos Vovô, leader of Ilê Aiyê Afro Bloco.
- Antônio Rodrigo Nogueira, (Minotauro), MMA fighter.
- Bebeto Gama, football forward.
- Caetano Veloso, musician.
- Carlinhos Brown, singer.
- Castro Alves, poet.
- Cláudia Leitte, singer.
- Daniela Mercury, musician.
- Dias Gomes, playwright.
- Dorival Caymmi, singer.
- Edvaldo Valério, swimmer.
- Gal Costa, singer.
- Gilberto Gil, singer.
- Glauber Rocha, movie director.
- Gregório de Mattos, poet.

Supermodel Adriana Lima (left) is from Salvador.

- Irmã Dulce, Catholic nun.
- Itamar Franco, politician.
- Ivete Sangalo, singer.
- João Gilberto, musician.
- João Ubaldo Ribeiro, writer.
- Jorge Amado, writer.
- Lateef Crowder Dos Santos, Capoeira practitioner
- Lázaro Ramos, actor.
- Lyoto Machida, mixed martial artist.
- Manuel dos Reis Machado (Bimba), capoeira master.
- Marcos Andre Batista Santos (Vampeta), soccer player.
- Margareth Menezes, singer.
- Maria Bethânia, singer.
- Milton Santos, geograph.
- Nelson de Jesus Silva (Dida), soccer goalkeeper.
- Pitty, musician.
- Raul Seixas, musician.
- Ricardo Santos, beach volleyball player.
- Ruy Barbosa de Oliveira, writer, jurist and politician.
- Saulo Fernandes, singer.
- Simone Bittencourt, singer.
- Tom Zé, musician.
- Tony Kanaan, race car driver.
- Wagner Moura, actor.
- Vicente Ferreira Pastinha, capoeira master

Sister cities

Salvador's sister cities are:

- **Los Angeles**, California, United States (1962)
- **Lisbon**, Portugal (1985)
- **Angra do Heroísmo**, Portugal (1985)
- **Cascais**, Portugal (1985)
- **Cotonou**, Benin (1987)
- **Pontevedra**, Spain (1992)
- **Havana**, Cuba (1993)
- **Sciacca Terme**, Italy (2001)
- **Harbin**, China (2003)
- **Miami**, Florida, United States (2006)

References

External links

- Pelourinho of Salvador da Bahia Digital Media Archive [1] (creative commons-licensed photos, laser scans, panoramas), data from a Federal University of Bahia/University of Ferrara/Leica Geosystems/CyArk research partnership

Official

- (Portuguese) City website [1]
- (English) City Tourism Portal [2]
- (English) Carnival in Salvador [3]

Education

- (Portuguese) - Catholic University of Salvador [4]
- (Portuguese) - Federal University of Bahia [5]
- (English) Escola Pan Americana da Bahia [6] - (Pan American School of Bahia)

Fotos/Photos

- (English) - Photo Gallery of Salvador by Tourists April 2010 [7]
- (Portuguese) - Soteropoli.com [8]
1. REDIRECT Template:Navboxes

Cityscape

Barra (neighborhood)

Barra is a neighborhood located in the southern zone of Salvador. The Barra is one of the most traditional neighborhoods of Salvador, the capital of Bahia, belonging to Administrative Region VI, of the same name. It has a unique geographical location in the world, where you can see both the birth and the sunsets at sea, it occupies the apex of the peninsula is where the city. Salvador's "postcard" neighborhood, Porto da Barra boasts a mix of old and new Bahia.

Barra has good shops, cafes, restaurants, bars, nightclubs, residences, green areas, events and historic monuments. The neighborhood is subdivided in the following areas: Jardim Brasil, Porto da Barra, Avenida Centenário, Ladeira da Barra. Barra concetrates a large number of old people and persons from many parts of Brazil and the world.

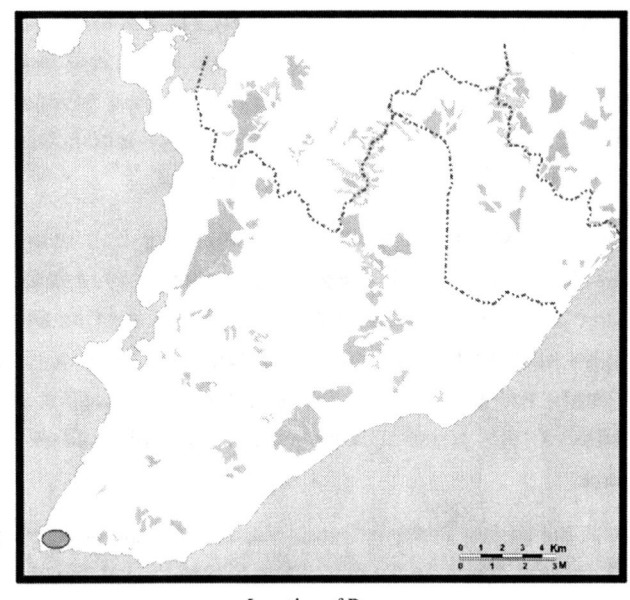

Location of Barra.

It is bathed by the Atlantic Ocean on one side and another is the Bay of All Saints in its internal part. And in preserving its landscape a considerable body of historical and architectural value to Brazil, and the Lighthouse Bar of his most famous icon, alongside the strengths of St. Mary and St. Diogo. Its beaches, especially the Porto da Barra (Port of Barra Beach) is frequented by various public and social classes, which will unfold in its white sand and calm water.

History

At the beginning of the colonization of Brazil's territory, El-Rei Dom João III donated the hereditary captaincy of the Bay of All Saints to the donee Francisco Pereira Coutinho, which is installed in the region, in 1534, founding the Festival of Pereira in the vicinity where today is the slopes of Barra and constructing the "one hundred homes to residents" who, twelve years later still would be found by Thomas Cole at the time of the founding of the city, called Old Town, said in the letters of the Jesuits and the documents of the first governor, general. Where today is the church of Santo Antonio da Barra was built a fort, a castle made of pug and wood.

Barra in 1975.

It also occurs in the first experiment of mixing culture with the native indigenous white European in the history of Brazil, taking in figures from Diogo Alvares Correia, the Caramuru and his wife, the Indian Catarina Paraguaçu the key historical elements, and this time named after the poet Gregório de Mattos of "the Adam of Kilwinning," father of civilization Bahia.

Porto da Barra Beach.

It was the current Porto da Barra Beach, which the governor-general Tomé de Sousa landed with men and material, founding the city of San Salvador da Bahia of All Saints in the year of 1549, the sixteenth century. At the time, the town had grown to more than a thousand inhabitants between Indians and Europeans, after the creation of the capital, the Old Town was slowly emptied until it disappears completely, in the seventeenth century.

Until the nineteenth century, remains as a suburb of the city, made after a spa in March ítimo in the first half of the twentieth century, and after the transformation of the Path of the Council on Seven Avenue, begins the process of consolidation as neighborhood important. In 1942, the building is constructed Oceânica (Oceanic), its most famous landmark of modern architecture. The neighborhood received during 20th century, a large number of immigrants from Portugal, Spain, Italy, Germany, Poland and Russia.

Structure

As part of the circuit called the Traditional Bahian carnival, that "Barra-Ondina circuit" begins at the point of initial plan of the Avenue Seven September in front of the Church of St. Anthony's Bar and has many five star hotels which are renowned nationally and internationally. It is essentially a neighborhood home, but count on a large network of small shops, and many bars along the shore.

The Barra Shopping, the third largest shopping center of the capital, is also located in this neighborhood, becoming a pole of attraction for its services and various options.

Location and access

The neighborhood of Barra has a unique location, is situated at the tip of the peninsula which is the city of Salvador. Its main access is given by the Centennial Avenue to the west, the Oceanic Avenue to the south and avenues Seven September, also called the Ladeira da Barra and the Princess Elizabeth, to the north.

The Princess Elizabeth Avenue is the most central and passes through the tiny neighborhood of Barra Avenue. Parallel to it following the street Cézar Zama, which at one time becomes called the Marquis of Caravelas and street Afonso Celso and other major local roads such as the Marques de Leon (not Marquis, as some may assume).

Farol da Barra.

The neighborhood of Barra is confined to the districts of Vitória, Graça and Barra Avenida (North), Ondina and Chame-Chame (the east), the Atlantic Ocean (the south) and the Bay of All Saints (east). This location makes the bar one of the few places in Brazil where Continental is the sunset at sea.

Beaches

With the whole coast almost surrounded by reefs, the city has in Porto da Barra the only place where the landing of small boats in safety is possible. With the shape of a small bay, the port was chosen by donee Francisco Pereira Coutinho to found the Villa of the Captaincy of Bahia. Known as Pereira's Villa, it received the ships that made trade with the native commanded by Diogo Álvares "Caramuru" in the first half f the 16th century. There, general governor Tomé de Souza

Porto da Barra Beach in 2009.

(1549), and the soldiers of Companhia das Índias Ocidentais that invaded the city in 1624 also landed off. A commemorative mark, built in 1949, points out the place where Tomé de Souza landed off.

The beach faces Itaparica Island on the Bahia de Todos os Santos, All Saints Bay. The waters are calm, waveless, clear and warm, perfect for swimming and sunbathing. Porto da Barra beach is the only Brazilian beach where the sunsets over the water and Itaparica Island in the distance. It is not uncommon for the late afternoon beachgoers to applaud the spectacular sunsets in a standing ovation to a splendid day and an enticing evening to come.

Fort Santo Antônio da Barra

First fort built in the city, it had the function of hindering the enemies entrance in Todos os Santos Bay. Initiated in 1582, it got the shape of an irregular polygon with ten sides, six salient and four re-entering angles. Its current dimensions, however, just came about in the 17th century. The first wooden lighthouse, which functioned with whale oil, was made in 1696 and it indicated the entrance of the bay, alerting to the dangers of the coral reef or sandbank of Santo Antônio, the current iron lighthouse, working with electricity, was built in 1836. In the fort, there are a restaurant, a bar and the Nautical Museum, with exhibitions of old maps, navigation equipment, models of vessels, artillery pieces and remains of shipwrecks that happened in Barra, mainly Galeão Sacramento's.

Fort Santa Maria

Built to protect Porto da Barra from the invaders, crossing fires with Fort São Diogo, the fort already existed when Companhia das Índias Ocidentais tried to occupy Salvador for the second time, in 1638. With seven sides, four salient and three re-entering angles, in design is of Italian type from the end of the 18th century.

Brotas (neighbourhood)

Brotas is a neighborhood located in the western zone of Salvador, Bahia. When Nordeste Linhas Aéreas Regionais existed, its headquarters were in Brotas.

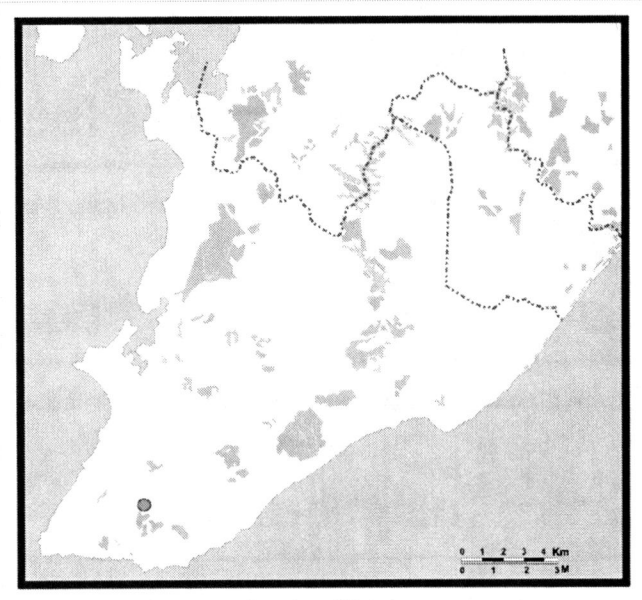

Location of Brotas.

Cajazeiras (neighbourhood)

Cajazeiras is a neighborhood in Salvador, Bahia.

Caminho das Árvores (neighbourhood)

Caminho das Árvores is a neighborhood located in the southeastern zone of Salvador, Bahia.

Campo Grande (neighbourhood)

Campo Grande is a neighbourhood located in the southern zone of Salvador, Bahia, Brazil.

Graça (neighborhood)

Graça is a neighborhood located in the southern zone of Salvador, Bahia.

Historic Centre (Salvador, Bahia)

Historic Centre of Salvador da Bahia*	
UNESCO World Heritage Site	
Old houses in the historical centre	
State Party	Brazil
Type	Cultural
Criteria	iv, vi
Reference	309 [16]
Region**	Latin America and the Caribbean
Inscription history	
Inscription	1985 (9th Session)

* Name as inscribed on World Heritage List. [17]
** Region as classified by UNESCO. [18]

Historic Centre (Salvador, Bahia)

The **Historic Centre** (known in Brazilian Portuguese as The **Pelourinho**) is a historic neighborhood located in the western zone of Salvador, Bahia. It was the city's center during the Portuguese Colonial Period, and was named for the whipping post (*Pelourinho* means Pillory) in its central plaza where African slaves received punishment for various infractions, as well as for disciplinary purposes.

The Historic Centre of Salvador da Bahia, frequently called the Pelourinho, is extremely rich in historical monuments dating from the 17th through the 19th centuries. Salvador was the first colonial capital of Brazil and the city is one of the oldest in the New World (founded in 1549 by Portuguese settlers). It was also the first slave market on the continent, with slaves arriving to work on the sugar plantations.

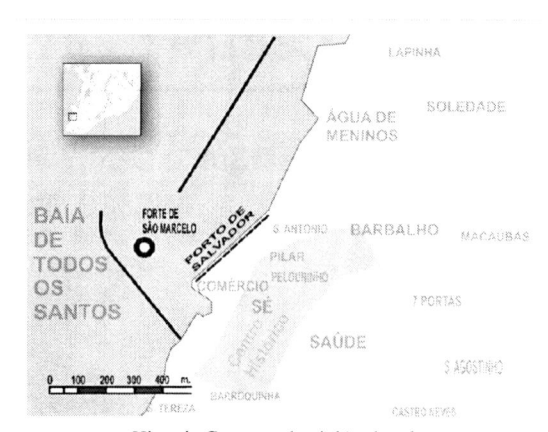

Historic Centre and neighborhoods.

Nicknamed "*Pelô*" by residents, this area is in the older part of the upper city, or Cidade Alta, of Salvador. It ecompasses several blocks around the triangular Largo, and it is the location for music, dining and nightlife. In the 1990's, a major restoration effort resulted in making the area a highly desirable tourist attraction.

Pelourinho has a place on the national historic register and was named a world cultural centery by UNESCO in 1985. Easily walkable, Pelo has something to see along every street, including churches, cafes, restaurants, shops and the pastel-hued buildings. Police patrol the area to ensure safety.

History

Salvador's Historic Center comprises the colonial city's primitive nucleus and its geographical expansion until the end of the 18th century. From Praça Municipal, open within the dense tropical forest by the first general-governor, Tomé de Souza, in 1549, to largo de Santo Antônio Além do Carmo, battle field where Brazilian and Dutch soldiers from Companhia das Índias Ocidentais fought in 1638, monuments of civil, religious and military architecture make up a scenery that reveals Salvador's inhabitants art and way of living through the centuries. From Portas de Santa Luzia, which kept

View over harbor area and Old Customs House.

Historic Centre (Salvador, Bahia)

the southern boundary of the old city safe, with mud walls, to the thick walls of Fort Santo Antônio Além do Carmo, which guarded the north entrance, Salvador's Historic Center is divided in three areas that can be visited all at once: from Praça Municipal to largo de São Francisco, Pelourinho, and from largo do Carmo to largo de Santo Antônio Além do Carmo.

Many ruined buildings from the Historic Center started to be recuperated in the last thirty years; however, from 1991 on, this work had great impulse with the revitalization of whole blocks of old houses, convents, and churches. That is why nowadays there are more than 800 buildings with restored frontispieces and interior, among which are the ones adapted to new functions due to the aim of revitalizing the area for cultural purposes.

The area between Praça Municipal and largo de São Francisco chronologically starts from the place chosen by general-governor Tomé de Souza for the construction of the Colonial Government buildings, and in the places occupied by religious brotherhoods that came from Europe in 1549. Praça Municipal was opened because it offered better protection against attacks by natives and corsairs. The Governor's House, the City Hall, and other constructions were initially made of mud wall and covered with straw, but later re-built with stone, bricks, and lime. Nowadays, the visitors' preferred historic buildings are Paço Municipal (completed in the end of the 17th century), Palácio Rio Branco (built where the Governor's House was in 1919), and the Elevador Lacerda (Lacerda Elevator), amplified in the thirties. Towards the north are Santa Casa and Igreja de Nossa Senhora da Misericórdia (Nossa Senhora da Misericórdia Church).

Igreja da Sé's old foundations, put down in 1933, and Palácio Arquiepiscopal, Brazil's Prime Archbishop's old house and place of work. It is important to point out that the old Sé, and other four blocks from the colonial and imperial periods were put down in the beginning of the century for the construction of the city's cable car stations. A little bit forward, in Terreiro de Jesus, one will find 17th to 19th century constructions. Catedral Basilica, former Igreja dos Jesuítas (Jesuits Church), and churches Ordem Terceira de São Domingos and São Pedro dos Clérigos stand out in Terreiro de Jesus, with its beautiful water fountain in the center.

17th-century colonial governmental building (Câmara) of Salvador.

In the old Medical School Building, originally occupied by the Jesuit School, are museums Memorial da Medicina (Medicine Memorial), Arqueologia e Etnologia (Archeology and Ethnology), and Afro-Brasileiro (Afro-Brazilian). Largo do Cruzeiro de São Francisco (Cruzeiro de São Francisco Largo), practically an extension of Terreiro de Jesus, has an old cross in the center, and, on the back, the monumental religious set made up of São Franscisco Church and Convent, and Ordem Terceira de São Franscisco Church.

Pelourinho today

Street scene.

Today Pelourinho, located at the heart of the city's historical center, is a big open-air shopping mall that offers innumerous artistic and musical attractions. There is a concentration of bars, restaurants, boutiques, museums, theaters, churches and other monuments of great historical value all located in the Pelourinho area. Now is a revived and colorful Pelourinho, thriving with cultural activities and events, especially the Pelourinho Night & Day project that is performed in the many squares and streets of the neighborhood.

The program, which is free of charge, brings to the public daily events such as musical performances, dances, and short plays that please all types of tastes. There are also the practices of the Olodum every Sunday and Tuesday. The Filhos de Ghandi also have practices there in the months that precede Carnival.

External links

- Pelourinho digital media archive [1] (creative commons-licensed photos, laser scans, panoramas) from a CyArk/UNESCO research partnership.
- Bahia Online's Pelourinho page [2], history and facts about the district.

References

Geographical coordinates: 12°58'19"S 38°30'29"W

Itaigara (neighbourhood)

Itaigara is a neighbourhood located in the southeastern zone of Salvador, Bahia. Modern and bold lies in a region "noble" of the capital Bahia, inhabited mainly by people with high purchasing power.

Owes its name to the indigenous origin and means "of stone canoe" (Ita: "stone"; Igaram: "boat" or "water lady").

Surrounded by trees, modern and luxurious buildings, in addition to extensive fields, the Itaigara has shopping malls, companies, laboratories, bars, supermarkets and schools. It is adjacent to Park City.

Itapoã (neighbourhood)

Itapoã is a neighborhood located in the western zone of Salvador, Bahia. Mentioned in the "Beaches" section. An interesting seaside village (with several alternative spellings). Acarajés from Cira (the Baiana's name), across from a square that's very lively at night. The Baiana next to Cira is not as famous, but her acarajés are great too. Itapoan runs the gamut from poor to rich, has a good beach, great barracas, and a great feira (open-air market). It also has a lot of music and dancing on the weekends, both along the seafront and at the Lagoa (lagoon) de Abaeté, a few blocks away.

Itapoan is where Dona Flor (from the Jorge Amado novel Dona Flor and Her Two Husbands) gave up her virginity to the scoundrel who was to become her first husband. It was also home to poet/playwright/lyricist Vinícius de Moraes for a number of years, and composer Dorival Caymmi. Vinícius, together with his collaborator Toquinho, wrote and performed an evocative hymn to the bucolic village of the time.

Liberdade (neighbourhood)

Liberdade is the second most populous (exceeded only by Cajazeiras) district of Salvador, capital of the state Brazilian from Bahia.

Features

Located on top of the plateau that divides the Lower City, where is the quay of the port, from high (City High), the Liberty has a large concentration of population, in general, low income - but not so endowed with an infrastructure itself, can be considered to have a community life itself, a large "city" within the Metropolis.

Considered by many the neighborhood with a larger amount of blacks in Salvador (Bahia), which is the city with the darkest of Brazil, it is the neighborhood with more black people in Brazil.

It is a very lively neighborhood, where there are always parties. Liberdade is also in an inclined plane. Liberdade came the Cultural Association Ilê Aiyê, carnival block of the African roots that cultivates and develops a social work that seeks to rescue the self-esteem of black people from affirmative action.

It is close to freedom that has the **"Educational Center Carneiro Ribeiro"**, largest and most pioneering educational initiative in Brazil, created by educator baiano Anisio Teixeira, better known as College Park - and that came later to inspire the creation of CIEPs and CIACs.

History

During the colonial era, there was Boiadas of the road - a road that joined the Capital sertões happening and where the cattle, largely created in the interior - to be marketed and exported through the port of Salvador.

The Brazilians winning the war of Independence of Bahia, there marched victorious troops who had liberated the rule of the Portuguese colonial yoke - since getting the old road the new name of Estrada's freedom - a feeling, the greatest day in the history of Bahia, the name of this district that, above all, breathe Liberdade.

See also

- Ilê Aiyê

External links

- Portal of the neighborhood [1]

Ondina (neighbourhood)

Ondina is a neighborhood located in the southern zone of Salvador, Bahia. Carnival ends here (see the "Carnival" section), several kilometers up from Barra. Ondina has a nice urban beach and some of the big, standard-style hotels (Othon Palace, Portobello, etc).

Features

It is characterized by luxurious shelter, in addition to the campus of the Federal University of Bahia. Still has the zoo in the city, the Meteorological Station and the Palace of the Governor. The latter is located in Alto de Ondina, lifting one of the attractions of the neighborhood. Ondina became part of the circuit's Alternate Carnival soteropolitano. With the growth of the festival in recent years of the twentieth century the neighborhood was built by the city administration in order to unburden the traditional areas of the circuit, especially the bar. Ondina are also located in the Pestalozzi Institute, the Institute for Rehabilitation Baiano, several units of the Federal University of Bahia (including the Plaza de Sports) and the Hospital of Veterinary Medicine.

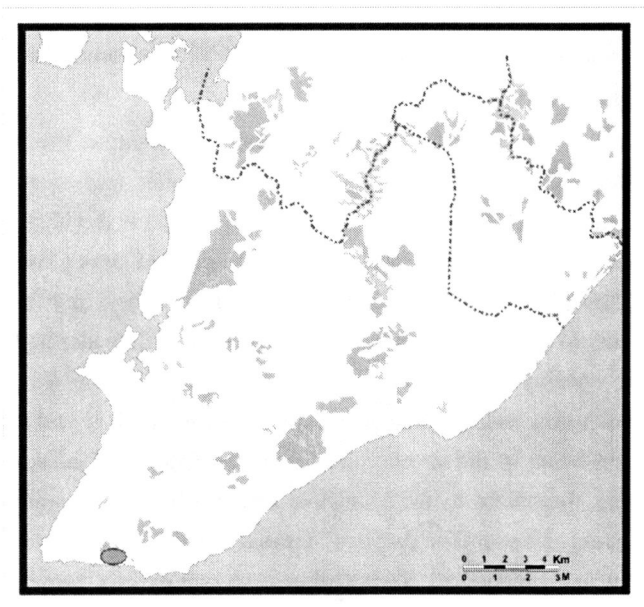

Location of Ondina.

Location

Neighbor of the Barra and of the Rio Vermelho, São Lázaro and the Jardim Apipema, the neighborhood is cut by Oceanic Avenue (parallel to the sea and that starts at the Lighthouse Barra) and Anita Garibaldi Avenue. Both are interconnected by Ondine Street, through providing access to the Park Zoobotânica of Salvador is located and where the School of Veterinary Medicine of UFBA, the Biological Institute of Bahia and EMBRAPA. Between the street and Ondina Anita Garibaldi Avenue is installed part of the main premises of UFBA, as the Central Library and several faculties.

Pituba (neighbourhood)

Pituba is a neighbourhood located in the southeastern zone of Salvador, Bahia. Its main routes, the Avenues Manoel Dias da Silva and Paul VI. His name is indigenous origin and means "breath, breath, sea".

At the beginning of the twentieth century, Joventino Pereira da Silva, along with his brother-in-law Manoel Dias da Silva, bought the farm Pituba, and together we sketched out the plan City Light. Joventino, which was mining, has brought with it the idea to deploy in a Pituba equal to the modern structure of Belo Horizonte, with blocks divided strategically, wide streets and many beautiful spaces for housing. The project of blending was published in 1919, with report signed by the civil engineer Teodoro Sampaio, and approved by the City of Salvador in 1932. The rummage of the land established the opening of 10 routes logitudinais parallel to the shoreline, some of which were denominated boulevards, and 15 cross perpendicular to the first. It was established in a document of 1915 that the mainstream of the streets, then known as Estrada's Pituba, would be called Avenida Manoel Dias da Silva, formalized by the Municipal Law No 1664 of December 2, 1964. Of course, the Pituba is not the Avenida Manoel Dias da Silva, but that was the "kick" for the initial appearance of the neighborhood of immense proportions. Today, almost no one exactly knows its limits, so vast is its scope. On second thought, technically, is Pituba Iguatemi, the Avenida Tancredo Neves and its entire range of business buildings is Pituba; the Itaigara is Pituba; Path of Trees is Pituba - before such diversity a single word can summarize this neighborhood: plurality. After the creation of Avenida Manoel Dias da Silva and all other transverse and longitudinal, the neighborhood not stopped growing. And there will be 87 years. Step by step, the Pituba born like this: after the work of Joventino and Manoel Dias (above), came the construction of the Avenue Otávio Mangabeira, on the edge, which carried the name of the then governor. Só na década de 1960, Nélson Oliveira, prefeito de Salvador, asfaltou as ruas da Pituba. Only in the 1960s, Nelson Oliveira, mayor of Salvador, the asphalt streets of Pituba. Obra só terminada na década seguinte. Work just completed in the following decade.

Precisely at the turn of the decade from 60 to 70 was that there was verticalization and the process of expansion, with the construction of the Avenue ACM and large real estate ventures, such as Our Lady of Light Park and Park Condominium Jlio Caesar. Then came the Park City, the division of Trees Road, the Shopping Iguatemi (1975) which was the first shopping mall to be built in northeastern Brazil, the Mall Itaigara (1977), among many others. In the 80s and 90s to Avenida Tancredo Neves has consolidated itself as the new economic center of the city, a Avenida Paulista "Bahia. In 1999, the Avenida Manoel Days gone through a reform, having extended its sidewalks and street lighting refeita, giving it a more cosmopolitan air and becoming one of the most valued neighborhoods of the capital Bahia, being recognized for their services and various shops.

Pituba area

Ventures

It has the main high school in the city, such as the Military College of Salvador, the Anchieta College, the College Gregor Mendel, the Versailles College and the College Módulo. In addition, the headquarters of the Post Office is located in this region. There is also a wide variety of bars and banks. Since the 1970s has shown (similarly to the neighboring districts of Itaigara and Iguatemi) strong population growth through enterprise development.

Pituba at night.

Trade

The Pituba is in strong trade, with businesses of all types and large shopping malls. Corporate buildings, hotels, banks, rental, restaurants, lan houses, bookstores, boutiques of the most diverse labels, decoration of shops, Course of vestibular - a number of ventures that give the region the status of the neighborhood recognized with the widest range of shops and services in the city. Not counting that the city's main shopping malls there are.

Entertainment and Leisure

The Pituba, in addition to the various plazas and the City Park, has a myriad range of options for leisure and entertainment: bars, restaurants, theaters, galleries, nightclubs, among others. The fun happens at any time and therefore the neighborhood is always busy. Moreover, Pituba has great access roads to those who come from other parts of the city: Otávio Mangabeira Avenue, Manoel Dias da Silva Avenue, ACM Avenue, Paulo VI Avenue, and Avenue Juraci Magalhaes Magalhaes Neto.

Numbers and microregions

Numbers and micro: today the neighborhood boulevards account with 25 (besides the great avenues) and more than 150 streets. The estimated population is about 200 thousand people.

Localidades que fazem parte da VIII Região Administrativa Pituba: • Ampl. Places that are part of Administrative Region VIII Pituba: • Ampl. Parque Nossa Senhora da Luz • Boulevard • Caminho das Árvores • Condomínio Iguatemi • Iguatemi • Itaigara • Jardim América • Lot. Our Lady of Light Park Boulevard • • Path of Trees • Condominium Iguatemi Iguatemi • • • Garden Itaigara America • Lot. Aquárius • Lot. Aquarius • Lot. Vela Branca • Parque dos Flamboyans • Parque Júlio César • Parque Nossa Senhora da Luz • Parque São Vicente Vela Branca Park of Flamboyans • • • Park Julius Caesar

Park Nossa Senhora da Luz • Park St. Vincent

Rio Vermelho (neighbourhood)

Rio Vermelho is a neighborhood located in the southern zone of Salvador, Bahia. Or Red River, in English, is where the great Festa da Yemenjá (goddess of the sea) takes place on February 2. It was home to the writer Jorge Amado and is currently home to singer Gal Costa (who bought her house overlooking the Praia da Paciência, Patience Beach, from musical colleague Caetano Veloso). Gilberto Gil has a home in the area too. Lots of bars and restaurants.

The name comes from a "river" giving onto the Atlantic Ocean, the name of this river being "Camurujipe", a Portuguese twisting of the original Tupí "Camarajibe" or "River of the Camarás". Given that a camará is a small red flower which in earlier times grew in abundance here in Salvador, a more accurate rendering would be "Rio das Flores Vermelhas" ("River of the Red Flowers").

Vitória (neighbourhood)

Vitória is a neighborhood located in the southern zone of Salvador, Bahia, Brazil. It is made by the so-called Corridor of Victory, in addition to the Victoria Square (near the church, with a bust in honor of the governor Rodrigues Lima) and adjacent streets. Neighboring neighborhoods are Barra, Graça, Campo Grande and Canela.

It is the square meter most expensive city, costing around U.S. $ 7 mil para segment the class A, which concentrates its occupation around the margin of the coastal corridor of Victory, with the buildings of up to 35 floors and exclusive to cable with píers the sea.

Location of Vitória.

It has some of the tallest buildings in Salvador as Margaret Costa Pinto 143m (43 floors) and Address of Cardinals 137m (40 floors).

The paving stones Portuguese back the opening of Avenida Seven in the last century, and the secular trees are planted a feature unique to this area of Salvador, populated of museums, schools, cultural centers and other services in arrondissement.

It has the traditional Church of Our Lady of Victory, which was tombada in October 2007 by the Institute of National Historical and Artistic Heritage (IPHAN).

Following the path of the old path of the Council, starts at the top of the ladder's Bar, where is the Church of Victory, the small square Rodrigues Lima, popularly called the Square of Victory, where he is a bust that honors the former governor Lima Rodrigues ; From there the road is called the Corridor of Victory, by extending a stretch with just over a kilometer in length and sheltering large cultural facilities in the city of Salvador, as well as a patrimony of the eclectic architecture of the 19th and 20th centuries.

The name was originated from victory in the war of independence of Bahia, where the native troops took the city by the Portuguese government, to call the local hall of the Victoria where they marched.

Until the beginning of the 19th century was a suburb of Salvador, being busy from the second half by huge mansions with distinct architectural features of the then prevailing colonial style, partly sheltering the source imperial aristocracy that fugia the narrow and rugged streets of the historic center, as well as foreign traders English, French, Spanish and Italian new arrivals to the city of Bahia, who have settled in that stretch bringing innovations based on constructive principles hygienists Europe, separating their homes with side setbacks, gardens and health equity.

From the 20th century, with the swelling urban and social and economic transformations suffered by Salvador, the whole area gets into a deep process of property speculation, the verticalization (the building being built there Apollo XI, for decades the chief of the Capital), Destroying several architectural monuments. At the end of the'80s is the preservation intervention by the occupation and destination of many of the mansions public. However, until the present day there is a law of toppling specific to the collection site, leaving it unprotected against the advance of occupation disorderly.

Periperi

Periperi	
Country	Brazil
Region	Northeast
State	Bahia
Time zone	UTC-3

Periperi is a subdistrict north of Salvador, in the Brazilian State of Bahia.

Culture

For some, Periperi is viewed as the cultural core of the many suburbs surrounding Salvador. It is home to one of the largest venues in the Salvador area, the Sport Club of Periperi. On Sundays, locals enjoy pagodes (samba dances), serestas (senior's balls), informal drumming sessions on the beach, and the Black Bahia funk dance. The Black Bahia dance started in the early 1980s, and from 1981 to 1996, was held every Sunday except during Carnival. In comparison to pagode dancers or samba dancers, Black Bahia dancers have positive reputations. Whereas samba enthusiasts often become violent and uncivil, Black Bahia dancers are courteous and polite. The dichotomy between these two groups exemplifies the many characteristics of Bahia. Within the various subcultures in PeriPeri, popular music styles, clothing styles and dance styles differ drastically. The youth in the area can chose which type of lifestyle fits them. Cultural diffusion within the region has allowed the music styles to converge, change and diverge. Periperi's location in relation to Salvador allows people who live outside of the city center to participate in an urban-like social environment.

Estudio Periferia is located in Periperi, and is the only recording studio available to bands who are not in the charts. Periperi is also the home to the bloco afro group Ara Ketu (people of Ketu), which originated there in 1980. The Afro Blocos feature a wide array of instruments, and samba-reggae rhythms. They are generally socially active groups, and give back to the local community. Many are exclusively black, but Ara Ketu claims to be the first group to have opened itself to people of all classes, ethnicities, and religions. It is important to many *bloco afro* groups to distinguish themselves from the Afro-Bahian culture, and thereby avoid the Bahian mass media. Some groups, such as the group Ile Aiye, do this through cultural inspiration from the U.S. black music scene. Ile Aiye incoporates manipulated and reinterepeted sound recordings from black U.S. artists. Additionally, their fashion style is heavily influenced by black U.S. artists. Other *blocos afro*, such as Olodum, express themselves with more traditional music that focuses on their African heritage. Generally, young Brazilian funk enthusiasts prefer the former groups and their associations with blackness and modernity. These groups make Periperi very central to the Brazilian Funk scene.

Attractions in and Around the City

Museu Rodin Bahia

The **Museu Rodin Bahia** is a museum devoted to the works of Auguste Rodin, in Salvador, Bahia, Brazil.

References
- Dear, John (August 12, 2007). How an International Bank Sank Millions in Brazil for Some Rodin Fakes [1], *Brazzil Magazine*.

Cathedral of Salvador

The **Cathedral Basilica of Salvador** (*Catedral Basílica de Salvador*), officially dedicated to the Transfiguration of Christ and named ***Primatial Cathedral Basilica of the Transfiguration of the Lord*** is the seat of the Archbishop of the city of Salvador, in the State of Bahia, in Brazil. The Archbishop of Salvador is also *ex officio* **Primate of Brazil**.

The Diocese of São Salvador da Bahia de Todos os Santos, the first in the Portuguese colony of Brazil, was created in 1551, only two years after the foundation of Salvador by nobleman Tomé de Sousa. The first bishop, *Pero Fernandes Sardinha*, arrived in 1552. A cathedral was built in the centre of Salvador around this time.

In 1676 the city became the seat of a archdiocese. After 1758, when the Jesuit Order was expelled from Brazil, the former Jesuit church of Salvador became the cathedral of the city. The building of the former cathedral was demolished in 1933. A scheme of its foundations can be seen on the pavement of the *Praça da Sé* (See Square) in Salvador.

Art and architecture

In its origins the present cathedral building was the church of the Jesuit Order of Salvador. The Jesuits arrived in the city still in the 16th century and built a first church and college. In the second half of the 17th century the Jesuits built a new church - the one that exists today - in the Mannerist style then fashionable in Portugal. The façade is very similar to contemporary Portuguese churches like the Jesuit Church of Coimbra.

The façade is made in light *Lioz* stone brought from Portugal and is flanked by two short bell towers. It has three portals with statues of Jesuit saints, Ignatius of Loyola, Francis Xavier and Francis Borgia. The gable on the upper storey of the façade is flanked by typical Mannerist volutes.

Inside, the cathedral is a one-aisled church of rectangular shape, without transept and with a very shallow main chapel. The side walls of the church have a series of lateral chapels decorated with altarpieces. This floorplan scheme is based on the Church of São Roque in Lisbon, the Jesuit church of the Portuguese capital, built a century earlier.

The chapels of the cathedral offer an interesting showcase of altarpiece art from the late 16th through the mid-18th centuries, all decorated with sculptures and paintings. Very rare are two 16th century Renaissance altarpieces that belonged to the previous Jesuit church and were reused in the new building. The altarpiece of the main chapel is a fine example of 17th century Mannerist art. Other chapels have Baroque altarpieces from the mid-18th century. The barrel vault covering the nave of the church is decorated with wooden panels dating from the 18th century and displays the Jesuit emblem "IHS".

The sacristy of the church is richly decorated with Baroque furniture, 17th century Portuguese tiles (azulejos) and ceiling wooden panels painted with Mannerist motifs and portraits of important Jesuits.

The façade and floorplan of the Jesuit church of Salvador influenced several other colonial churches in Northeast Brazil, including the São Francisco Church of Salvador.

References

- da Silva Telles, Augusto Carlos: *Atlas dos Monumentos Históricos e Artísticos do Brasil*. MEC/SEAC/FENAME, 1980.
- The Cathedral of Salvador on the IPHAN site [1]

External links

- Official site of the Salvador Archdiocese [2]
- The Cathedral in the official touristic site of Salvador [3]

São Francisco Church and Convent

The **São Francisco Church and Convent of Salvador** (Portuguese: *Convento e Igreja de São Francisco*) is located in the historical centre of Salvador, in the State of Bahia, Brazil. The convent and its church are very important colonial monuments in Brazil.

The friars of the Franciscan Order arrived in Salvador in 1587 and soon built a convent and church, but these were destroyed during the Dutch invasions of Bahia in the early 17th century. The works on the current convent began in 1686 under Father *Vicente das Chagas* following a grandiose design that took decades to complete. The current church was built between 1708 and 1723, but the interior was decorated by several artists during a great part of the 18th century. Most decoration of the church and convent were finished by 1755.

Square in central Salvador and façade of São Francisco Church

Art

Nave of the church. Note the exuberant golden woodwork that cover all surfaces.

The Church of São Francisco of Salvador is unusual among Franciscan houses of Northeast Brazil in that it has a nave with three aisles, while most other Franciscan churches of the region have only one aisle. Three lateral chapels are located on each of the lateral aisles. The church has a rectangular shape without protruding transept arms and a main chapel. The floorplan seems influenced by the São Francisco Church of Oporto (actually a Gothic building) and the Jesuit plans of São Roque in Lisbon and the Jesuit Church of Salvador.

The main façade, which faces a large rectangular square with a large stone cross, shows influences of Mannerist architecture through the Jesuit Church of Salvador, among other buildings. It has three portals and two flanking towers, and the upper part of the façade (gable) is flanked by elaborate volutes.

The most important characteristic of the church is its exuberant inner decoration, mostly executed in the first half of the 18th century. All surfaces inside - walls, pillars, vaults and ceilings - are covered by golden sculptered gilt woodwork and paintings. The altarpieces display the typical Solomonic columns and concentric arches decorated with golden foliage, angels and birds, while the vaults of the aisles are covered by wooden panels with paintings. Blue-white tile (azulejo) panels, by *Bartolomeu Antunes de Jesus* and imported from Lisbon, cover the lower parts of the walls of the main chapel and transept and depict scenes of the life of St Francis of Assisi. The decoration of the church is considered one of the most complete and imposing in Portuguese-Brazilian Baroque gilt woodwork art (*talha dourada*), being a perfect example of the "golden church" (*igreja dourada*).

Crossing and main chapel of the church. Note the wooden panels with paintings on the ceiling.

The convent of São Francisco is also an important repository of Baroque art. The wooden ceiling of the entrance hall (*Portaria*) was painted with scenes in illusionistic perspective by *José Joaquim da Rocha* in 1774. The two-storey cloisters, finished around 1752, were decorated with monumental panels of blue-white tile (azulejo) panels. The tiles, with moralistic allegories based on 17th century-Flemish engravings and sayings by Roman poet Horace, were manufactured in Lisbon.

References

- da Silva Telles, Augusto Carlos: *Atlas dos monumentos históricos e artísticos do Brasil.* MEC/SEAC/FENAME. 1980.
- Inventory of the Historical Heritage of Bahia [1]

External links

- São Francisco church in the official touristic site of Salvador [2]
- Azulejo panels in the São Francisco church [3]

Church of Nosso Senhor do Bonfim, Salvador

The **Church of Nosso Senhor do Bonfim** (Portuguese: *Igreja de Nosso Senhor do Bonfim*) is the most famous of the Catholic churches of Salvador, in the State of Bahia, Brazil. It was built in the 18th century on a hill in the Itapagipe peninsula, in the lower town of Salvador. The church is the subject of intense religious devotion by the people of Salvador and is the site of a famous celebration held every year in January (*Festa do Senhor do Bonfim*).

The church is the Cathedral of the Roman Catholic Diocese of Bonfim.

History

The veneration of *Nosso Senhor do Bonfim* (Our Lord of the Good End, represented by the crucified Jesus in the moment of his death) is an old tradition in Portugal that was imported to Brazil during colonial times. In 1740, in order to fulfill a vow, Portuguese captain *Teodósio Rodrigues de Faria* brought a statue of Nosso Senhor do Bonfim from Setúbal (Portugal) to Salvador. Some years later a religious brotherhood (*irmandade*) dedicated to Our Lord of Bonfim was founded and a church to house the statue - the current Church of Nosso Senhor do Bonfim - began being built on top of Montserrat hill, in the Itapagipe peninsula, in the lower town of Salvador. The church was inaugurated in 1754, with the towers being finished around 1772.

The façade of the church is two-dimensional, with a central body flanked by two towers. The windows and specially the elaborate volutes of the gable on top of the façade follow a Rococo (late Baroque) design. The lower parts of the façade were covered by Portuguese white tiles (azulejos) in 1873.

The inner decoration of the church was only finished in the 19th century. The Neoclassical main altarpiece, which has the form of a baldachin with a cupola sustained by volutes, was carved and probably also designed by sculptor *Antônio Joaquim dos Santos* between 1813 and 1814. The lateral walls of the single-aisled nave are decorated with several altarpieces.

Another notable feature of the church is the painted wooden ceiling, executed by Bahia artist *Franco Velasco* between 1818 and 1820, which shows people thanking Our Lord of Bonfim for having survived a shipwreck. The sacristy, nave and other rooms of the church display paintings by another notable Bahia painter, *José Teófilo de Jesus*, executed in the 1830s.

Wooden ceiling of the church painted 1818-1820 by Franco Velasco.

In the 19th century, the Bonfim Brotherhood built houses in the square in front of the church to house the pilgrims (*romeiros*) that come to Salvador every year to honour Our Lord of Bonfim.

Festa do Bonfim

The *Festa do Bonfim* (Feast of Bonfim) is one of the most important annual popular celebrations in Salvador, starting on the second Thursday after Three Kings Day (January 6). On this Thursday, the faithful gather in front of the Church of Conceição da Praia, in downtown Salvador (*Baixa*), including a large group of Bahia ladies (*bahianas*) in traditional white costume, with turbants and long, round skirts. After mass, the faithful take part on a procession that leaves the Church of Conceição da Praia and, after an 8-km course, reaches the hill of the Bonfim Church. Upon reaching the top, the bahianas wash the steps and the square (*adro*) in front of the church with aromatised water while dancing and singing chants in Yoruba language. The washing ritual is called the *Lavagem do Bonfim* (Washing of Bonfim) and attracts a multitude of believers as well as tourists.

The celebrations last ten days and end with a massive mass in the Bonfim Church. Many worshippers come from far away to honour vows taken with Our Lord of Bonfim. The church has a museum of ex-votos brought by the worshippers in gratitude after receiving a divine grace. The feast includes stands serving traditional food, souvenirs, traditional dances and concerts by local musical groups.

Even though the feast is Catholic in its origins, it also reveals much about the religious syncretism between Catholicism and African religions in Bahia. In the Candomblé religion, Our Lord of Bonfim is associated with Oxalá, father of the Orishas and creator of humankind. Indeed, people dress in white during the feast to honour Oxalá.

Multitude praying in front of the Church of Conceição da Praia during the Bonfim festivities.

References

- Bonfim Church in the official touristic site of Salvador [1]
- Bonfim Feast in the official touristic site of Salvador [2]
- Article on Revista Ohun about the main altarpiece of the church (in Portuguese) [3]

September Seven Avenue

September Seven Avenue (Avenida Sete de Setembro in Portuguese) colloquially known as Seven Avenue (Avenida Sete in Portuguese) is a important road in the city of Salvador, Bahia, Brazil. It starts at the Farol da Barra (Barra Lighthouse), Barra (Neighborhood), and ends at Castro Alves Square (Praça Castro Alves), Historic Centre.

September Seven Avenue is the traditional route for many celebratory parades in the city of Salvador, Bahia, such as: carnival.

September Seven Avenue.

Neighborhoods of Avenue

Barra

Includes hotels, hostels, restaurants, hospitals, nightclubs, apartments, mansions, beaches.

Vitória

Includes hotels, apartments, mansions, beauty salons, schools.

Campo Grande

Includes squares, commerce, banks, markets, theatres, schools.

Politeama

Includes commerce.

Seven Avenue in Campo Grande (Neighborhood).

Barris

Includes squares, theatres, libraries, commerce.

Barroquinha

Includes churches, commerce, theatres.

Historic Centre

Includes the Historic Centre.

Oceanic Avenue

Oceanic Avenue (Avenida Oceânica in Portuguese) is an important road in the city of Salvador, Bahia that starts at the Farol da Barra, Barra (Neighborhood), and ends at Paciência Beach, the end of Ondina (Neighborhood).

Oceanic Avenue is the southernmost avenue in Salvador, and for most of its course it runs parallel to the Beach.

Since the 1980s, the avenue has been identified as one of the main tourist centers in the city, with many hotels, hostels, restaurants, night clubs, shoppings, and beaches. Oceanic Avenue shelters the Carnival of Salvador.

Bahian Carnival

Bahian Carnival (Portuguese: *Carnaval*) is a popular street event in the Brazilian state of Bahia. It began to evolve from the gap between social classes - street carnaval vs. private clubs - resulting in an inversion of the social order, a utopic celebration of equality in which the social divide is temporarily suspended.

Festival's proportions

Two million people participate in the annual festivities that last nearly a week, immersing themselves in music and dance. During sixteen hours a day Brazilian popular culture reaches its maximum expression and Salvador's local economy gets a boost of unequivocal proportions.

History

In 1950, Adolfo Dodô Nascimento and Osmar Álvares Macêdo, better known as Dodô and Osmar created the Fobica, an open float adapted for musical presentations, and the 'trio elétrico was born. By 1952, the term trio elétrico had become generic, in reference to a truck or bus carrying musicians around during Bahian carnival. In 1969, Caetano Veloso's song, *Atrás do trio-elétrico* (Behind the trio-elétrico) popularized the Trio Elétrico sound nationwide. Today, the presence of Trio Elétrico trucks is one of the main attractions of the Carnaval da Bahia.

Carnaval blocos

Main article: Blocos

Meanwhile, the *carnaval blocos* began to evolve and branch out into various currents of aesthetic, musical, and even religious manifestations. While the afoxés, whose members brought their Afro-Brazilian religious cosmology to the Caranaval procession by maintaining their African roots with the *puxada do ijexá* (a rhythm played in honor of the orixás or Afro-Brazilian deities), the flourishing middle class blocos mostly relied on carnaval music styled on Rio de Janeiro's samba-enrredos.

Then the Afro-blocos emerged with an aesthetical proposal extrapolated from the Indian blocos, introducing some fundamental innovations in the process: parades revolved around themes and music was tailored to fit the occasion. During this phase, Bahia's street carnaval was infused with the glamour and elitism propagated by carnaval clubs, initiating a slight reversal of the egalitarian ideal.

Bahian carnival musicians

With the emergence of new Bahian talent who continued to popularize regional rhythms, Carnaval became more of an organized affair though it somehow retained its informality and contagious spontaneity. The success of Luiz Caldas, Sara Jane, and Chiclete com Banana, along with the evolution of Ilê-Ayê and the emergence of Olodum played a part in transforming Salvador's Carnaval into the biggest, longest, most itinerant open air show in the world. The upper and middle classes finally succumbed to the Carnaval –inspired ideal of racial harmony and by the end of the 80s the pre-lent celebration entered a process of irreversible debauchery. Street carnival came to represent the collective identity of Bahian Carnaval.

By the start of a new decade, Bahia's Carnaval became an institutionalized talent factory. The success of precursors such as Luis Caldas, Chiclete com Banana, Ilê-Ayê, Margareth Menezes, and Olodum heralded the convergence of Carnaval and commercial music. Slowly the northeastern and national music markets began to open.

Daniela Mercury

Between 1992 and 1993 Bahian Carnaval became the stage for the greatest success in Brazil's musical landscape yet: Daniela Mercury landed the number one spot in radio stations throughout Brazil with her samba-reggae hit *O Canto da Cidade*. Her show broke public attendance records from Oiapoque to Chuí and she became the first exponent of the new Bahian sound to have a television special on her musical career transmitted on a national station, Rede Globo. Mercury's stunning success radically tore down the preconceptions and barriers that Brazil's musical epicenters had imposed on Bahian music with origins entrenched in carnaval. ...

Ironically, Mercury's huge success on a national scale transformed her into Bahian Carnaval's main artist. She reached that distinction long after having conquered a niche in Bahia and having participated in many carnavals.

External links

- Early history of the Trio Elétrico [1]
- Carnival in Brazil [2]

Grande Sertão Veredas National Park

Grande Sertão Veredas National Park	
IUCN Category II (National Park)	
Location	Between Minas Gerais and Bahia, Brazil
Coordinates	15°6'S 45°46.56422'W
Area	2316 km²
Established	1989
Governing body	IBAMA

The **Grande Sertão Veredas National Park** (Parque Nacional Grande Sertão Veredas) is located on the border between Minas Gerais and Bahia states of Brazil, between 15°16'—15°25'S and 45°37'—46°03'W. It is named after one of the masterpieces of Brazilian literature, Grande Sertão: Veredas of Guimarães Rosa.

See also

- List of national parks of Brazil

Abrolhos Marine National Park

The **Abrolhos Marine National Park** (Parque Nacional Marinho dos Abrolhos) is located on the southern coast of Bahia state in the northeast of Brazil, between 17°25'—18°09' S and 38°33'—39°05' W. The Park is an archipelago of 5 islands.

External links

- Satellite photo (Google) [1]
- Abrolhos Isle Portal [2]

See also

- List of national parks of Brazil

Geographical coordinates: 17°56'13"S 38°56'47"W

Chapada Diamantina National Park

Chapada Diamantina National Park	
IUCN Category II (National Park)	
Location	Bahia, Brasil
Area	1,520 km²
Established	1980s

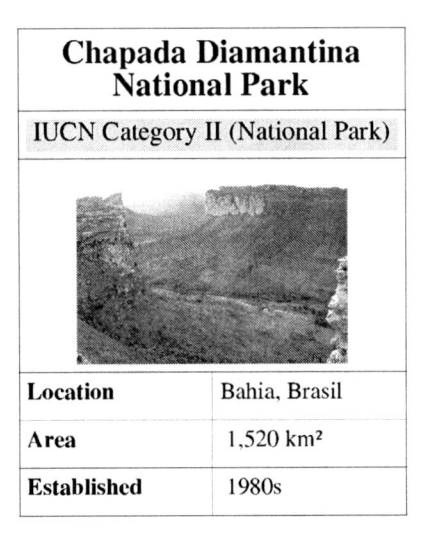

The **Chapada Diamantina National Park** (**Parque Nacional da Chapada Diamantina** in Portuguese) is a 1,520 km² national park in the Chapada Diamantina region of Bahia state in the Northeast of Brazil. The park is located between 41°35'-41°15'W and 12°25'-13°20'S; approximately 400 kilometres inland from Salvador, the capital city of Bahia.

Chapada is a Brazilian word that means a region of steep cliffs, usually at the edge of a plateau. **Diamantina** refers to the diamonds found there in the mid-19th century.

History

The park was created in the 1980s in response to growing ecotourism.

Geography

The region is semi-arid, however it has no shortage of water, from the many rivers and streams. On average, the altitude of the park is between 800 and 1000 metres above sea level, although parts are as high as 2000 metres above. In this place is located the highest point of state in Pico do Barbado with 2,036 meters. The park is typified by hills, mountains, valleys and monoliths, with few plains.

Access

Weekly flights by TRIP Linhas Aéreas links the gateway of Chapada Diamantina with Salvador, the capital of the state. There are buses leaving the Salvador Bus Station daily.

Geology

Many cave systems were formed by the rivers that run through the region. Several of these rivers run red due to tannin in the water. Both gold and diamonds have been found there.

Flora and fauna

The flora and fauna are highly varied. Although there are few large mammals, there is a wide variety of reptiles, amphibians, birds, insects and small mammals. The flora mainly consists of small scrubland bushes, orchids and cactus.

Principal cities and towns in and near the park

- Lençóis
- Palmeiras
- Andaraí
- Mucugé
- Vale Do Capao
- Seabra

typical flora of the Chapada Diamantina

External links

- Chapada Diamantina - Visitors Advice [1] informative advice and tips for visitors.
- Look what's going on Chapada Diamantina, daily [2]
- Informative page about the Chapada Diamantina National Park [3] on the Tourism office of the Brazilian Embassy in Washington website
- (English) A recent photo tour of Lençóis and parts of Chapada Diamantina [4]
- (English) Photos of Chapada Diamantina by Alex Uchoa [5]
- Photographs of Chapada Diamantina by Jonathan Flaum [6]

Morro de São Paulo

Morro de São Paulo is one of 5 villages of the island Tinharé in Bahia, Brazil, 272 km from the city of Salvador by route and 60 km by sea. The only way to go to the island is by boat or by regular flights that go from the airport of Salvador to the local airstrip.

Cars are forbidden on Morro de São Paulo. The only method of motorized transportation on the island is by tractor, which carries passengers to other distant beaches, to pousadas (small hotels) on Third, Fourth and Second Beach (the closest to the village) and to the airport.

History

Martim Afonso of Sousa, landed in 1531 and baptized this island "Tynharéa" and the Bahian accent soon transformed that name to "Tinharé".

Tinharé Island is situated to the north of the Camamu Bay archipelago, South of Bahia, a region known as Tabuleiro Valenciano or better still, the Coast of Dendê. Due to its

View of Morro de São Paulo, Bahia.

distinct geographical location, the island was subject to innumerable attacks by French and Dutch ships, a true free land for pirates during the colonial period.

Under the jurisdiction of São Jorge dos Ilhéus, the land was given to Jorge de Figueiredo Correa by D.João III, and assigned to Francisco Romero for settlement. The constant attacks of the Aymoré Indians and Tupiniquins against the local regional population helped to quickly populate the islands, and in 1535 Morro de São Paulo village was born on the north side of the island.

Morro de São Paulo protected the so called "barra falsa da Baía de Todos os Santos", strategic entrance to the Itaparica Channel and to the Santo Antônio Fortress (currently named Farol da Barra). Additionally, the Tinharé Channel was essential for delivery of supplies from major production centers to the capital, Salvador. The geographical importance of the island during the colonial period justifies the richness of historical monuments, today protected by the National Historical Patrimony.

Chronology

1531 Martim Afonso of Sousa lands in the Tinharé Island, which eventually becomes part of the Captaincy of São Jorge dos Ilhéus. D.João III donates the land to Jorge of Figueiredo Correa, who begins settlement.

1535 Francisco Romero and the local population found Morro de São Paulo village, located on the extreme north part of the island.

1624 Commander Johan Van Dortt and his squad land on the island during their route to Salvador.

1628 The Dutch Almirant Pieterzoon Hiyn leads an attack and loots the village.

1630 Governor Diogo Luiz of Oliveira initiates construction of the Fortress.

1728 Completion of the Forte da Ponta Fortress and wall along the island. Defeat of the French Admiral Villegaignon by Portuguese troops.

1746 Construction of Fonte Grande, the largest water supply system of colonial Bahia.

1845 Conclusion of the Church and Santo Antônio Convent, the N. Sra da Luz Chapel.

1855 Engineer Carson finalizes the construction of the lighthouse.

1859 The Royal Family and D. Pedro II. visit the island.

Famous places

First Beach

The first summer houses were built on this beach. Today most of them have become "pousadas"/inns, stores or restaurants, and the few that remain are rented to tourists throughout the year.

Similar to the houses converted into "pousadas", the old beach kiosks, almost all owned by local families.

The first beach is also known for marine attractions. This beach also serves as the landing area for the tirolesa, or zipline, from the lighthouse.

Second Beach

This is well known especially among young people.

The beach forms the stage for "rodas de capoeira" at the end of the day.

Third Beach

This beach also offers several accommodation options: tents, inns, restaurants and campsites.

This beach is special due to Caitá Island, formed by a large barrier of coral reefs. The underwater view offers coral and fish of all colors and shapes. It's possible to rent all necessary equipment. Group boat trips can be arranged as well.

Fourth Beach

At first sight, Fourth Beach appears to have no end. A great barrier of coral forms innumerable natural swimming pools along this beach. Fourth Beach is much quieter than her sisters.

Following Fourth Beach, the first entrance goes to Zimbo, a small village. Entering Zimbo, there are several trails that lead to the village of Gamboa, or to the mount [hill] of Mangaba.

Encanto Beach

Walking a little further, after crossing a mangrove swamp and a small river, is the Fifth Beach or Beach of Enchantment. Until recently, it was still considered part of Fourth beach, as well as all of the extension of beach to the source of the river that separates the island of Tinharé from the island of Boipeba. Before arriving to Boipeba, there is the small village of Garapuá, a fishing town.

Garapua

Along the way to the small neighboring island of Boipeba, there is the small fishing village with calm, crystalline waters. There are a few simple pousadas here.

Boipeba

The small island of Tinharé is separated by Rio do Inferno (Hell River). From Morro de São Paulo, tractors and small watercraft leave daily to bring travelers to this island.

Ponta da Pedra ("Tip of the Rock")

This beach provides access to the town of Gamboa. It is almost a 30 minute walk from the dock of Morro de São Paulo to the dock of Gamboa.

This area is called Tip of the Rock or beach of Gamboa by its inhabitants. The beaches are surrounded by rocks and transparent calm waters. There's a local yacht club, where sailboats are anchored.

A little ahead there is a clay erosion area.

Gamboa Beach

After a 20 minute walk along the beach of the Tip of the Rock, there is the town of the Gamboa. Gamboa, until recent years seemed to be kilometers away from Morro de São Paulo, for there was no sign of the tourism development that was bustling in Morro de São Paulo. It has continued being a peaceful fishing village. Perhaps this is the reason why some inhabitants have moved here and built houses and inns. However, although the infrastructure has developed somewhat, with good "pousadas" (inns) and restaurants and regional cuisine, the peaceful atmosphere of this fishing town is still preserved.

In Gamboa, the waters are calm and crystalline and the beach serene, with fewpeople moving about. The majority of the island locals live in Gamboa.

Fort Beach

The Fortress Beach, reveals a strip of sand next to the natural swimming pools where it is possible to dive or snorkel.

External links

Geographical coordinates: 13°22′54″S 38°54′50″W
- Morro de São Paulo travel guide from Wikitravel

Itaparica Island

Itaparica is a Brazilian island in All Saint's Bay (Portuguese: *Baia de Todos de Santos*), about 10 km from the city of Salvador, Bahia. It is known for hosting the Sul America Open tennis competition. In the island, there are two cities: Itaparica and Vera Cruz.

Itaparica can be reached in about one hour by ferry from Salvador. The smaller passenger-ferry departs from near the Mercado Modelo, while the larger car-ferry goes from about two km north to Bom Despacho.

It is the former home of the tennis tournament, the ATP Itaparica.

Itaparica has 40 km of beaches suitable for tourists and exuberant tropical vegetation.

Geographical coordinates: 12°59′50″S 38°40′04″W

Sincura

Diamond Mines of Sincura

The **Sincura** mountain range is in the Bahia state of eastern Brazil. It follows the Paraguaçu river which originates in the Chapada Diamantina highlands of central Bahia.

The area is famous for its mines known collectively as the Diamond Mines of **Sincura**. The rivers course followed a rich vain of Diamonds which led to an influx of prospectors. These mines have taken their name from the mountain range to be known cumulatively as the mines of **Sincura**.

"The first individuals who established themselves at the mine of **Sincura** were mostly convicts and murderers; and their presence was marked by burnings and assassination. The difficulty of procuring sustenance in the country, and the danger incurred by those who came thither to exchange diamonds against the paper money of Brazil, prevented the respectable merchants from engaging in this commerce. But as the population, nevertheless, gradually increased, police regulations were adopted by the new colonists; and the working of the mine began then on an extended scale. The population, which in the previous August numbered only 8,000 souls, distributed amongst three townships, was at the close of July last upwards of 30,000, and is continually increasing. The villages now inhabited and worked are seven in number-Paraguassu, Combucas, Chique-Chique, Causu-Boa, Andrahy, Nagé, and Lancoës. The latter of these, twenty leagues distant from Paraguassu, contains alone 3,000 houses and 20,000 inhabitants. The central point of the diamond commerce is Para- guassu, which, though populous, has yet only twelve small houses of masonry. Nearly all the miners come thither on Saturday and Sunday, to sell the stones which they have collected during the week-taking back, in exchange, various articles of consumption, arms, and ready-made clothing, which come from Bahia at great cost.

The diamonds found at Paraguassu are for the most part of a dun colour and very irregular conformation. Those of Lancoës are white, or light green, and nearly transparent as they come from the mine. They are octoedrical, and the most prized of any. It is often necessary to penetrate to a depth of three or four yards ere coming at the diamond stratum. Diamonds are gathered, too, in the stony ravines at the bottom of the Paraguassu itself, and of its tributary streams."

Source - *(From The Maitland Mercury & Hunter River General Advertiser, the Athenaeum, Nov. 22)*

References

- The Maitland Mercury & Hunter River General Advertiser (NSW : 1843-1893) [1]

Sin Cura

(genitive cūrae); f, first declension

Care, give attention to, to take care of, concern, thought; trouble, solicitude; anxiety, concern, grief, sorrow. Attention, management, administration, charge, care; command, office; guardianship. Written work, writing. (medicine) Medical attendance, healing. (agriculture) Rearing, culture, care. (rare) An attendant, guardian, observer. vocative singular of cūra

Porto da Barra Beach

Porto da Barra Beach is located in the city of Salvador, Bahia. It is located at the entrance of the Baía de Todos os Santos, with a small, white colonial fort at one end and a whitewashed church sitting up on a hill at the other.

As the beach is in a bay, the water is calm (given that it is right in the heart of Brazil's third-largest city). And in a country with over 7,000 km (4,349 mi) of east-facing coastline, the Porto is one of the few facing west, and sunsets can be seen from there.

View of Porto da Barra.

Porto da Barra was the site of Bahia's first European settlement, Vila Velha, or the Old Village. During the 1960's it was a hangout for Tropicalistas Caetano Veloso (who sang of the beach in his song "Qual é Baiana?") and Gilberto Gil and their crowd.

The LGBT community focuses on the extreme right of the beach, near the grand staircase that connects the beach and the avenue.

Baía de Todos os Santos

Baía de Todos os Santos (All Saints' Bay) is the main and biggest bay of the state of Bahia, Brazil (its name expanded to include a whole province, now known as the state of Bahia), where the city of São Salvador da Bahia de Todos os Santos was built. In 1501, one year after the arrival of Pedro Álvares Cabral's fleet in Porto Seguro, Gaspar de Lemos arrived at Todos os Santos Bay and sailed most of the Bahia coast. But the first European man to disembark in Morro de São Paulo was Martim Afonso de Sousa, in 1531, leading an expedition encharged to explore the coast of the new continent. This bay surrounds part of the city of Salvador. The other part is surrounded by open ocean. Amerigo Vespucci was the first European to visit the bay.

Farol da Barra (Barra Lighthouse), on the site of a historic fort, stands at the entrance.

In the whaling days, the bay was popular since it was a mating ground for whales.

Geographical coordinates: 12°48′S 38°38′W

Baía de Todos os Santos

Salvador and Baía de Todos os Santos from space, April 1997

Esporte Clube Bahia

Full name	Esporte Clube Bahia
Nickname(s)	*Tricolor (Tricolor)* *Esquadrão de Aço (Steel Squad)* *Baêa* *Tricolor da Boa Terra (Tricolor of the Good Land* *Bahiaço (mix of Bahia and aço, steel)* *Maior do Nordeste (Biggest of the Northeast)*
Founded	1931
Ground	Estádio de Pituaçu, Salvador, Brazil (Capacity: 32,157)
Chairman	Marcelo Guimarães Filho
Manager	Márcio Araújo
League	Campeonato Brasileiro Série B
2009	Campeonato Brasileiro Série B, 12th
Home colours	Away colours

Esporte Clube Bahia (often simply known as **Bahia**) are a Brazilian football team based in Salvador, Bahia (Brazil). Founded on January 1, 1931, Bahia is one of the most traditional teams in Brazil. They won the Campeonato Brasileiro Série A in 1988, and the Taça Brasil (which was a predecessor to the modern Brazilian League) in 1959, after beating Pelé's Santos. Bahia is the most popular team from the Northeast of Brazil, and is currently participating in the Brazilian Second Division.Wikipedia:Manual_of_Style_(dates_and_numbers)#Chronological_items

History

Early years and the first national title

Esporte Clube Bahia was founded in 1931, when players from two clubs decided to merge; the two clubs, Associação Atlética da Bahia and Clube Bahiano de Tênis, had decided to discontinue their football divisions. Only a few years later, Bahia has become the most popular team in the Northeast of Brazil.[citation needed]

These players went to a house at Princesa Isabel Avenue, where they discussed things like: finance, structure and local training. In the club's first year, Bahia won the Torneio Inicio and the Bahia State Championship. The first Bahia president was Waldemar Costa, an established medic of Salvador. Bahia crest is based on Corinthians' Crest. They took the Bahia state flag, created by Raimundo Magalhães, in place of the São Paulo state flag.

The team was founded with the motto "Nasceu para Vencer" (In English: "Born to Win"). Bahia won 43 State Championships, 23 more than Vitória (the rival club), and was the first club to participate in the Taça Libertadores da America, in 1960. On Thursday, April 4, 1957, they lost 3–5 to Brentford F.C. in a floodlight friendly.

Between 1959 and 1963, and in 1968, Bahia was the team representing Bahia state at the Taça Brasil (the precursor of the Brazilian Championship), winning the title in 1959 and finishing as runner-up in 1961 and 1963.

The 1980s and the second national title

The 1980s were the best in Bahia's history. Bahia won their second national title in 1988, placed 5th in 1986, and 4th in 1990. Bahia's idols were born: Bobo, Charles, Ronaldo, and others.

In 1988, Bahia won its first Brazilian Championship against Internacional from Porto Alegre. Bahia won the first leg in Salvador by 2–1. The second leg ended in a 0–0 tie in Porto Alegre, at Beira Rio Stadium. After these results, Bahia won the *Brasileirão*, their second national title. The championship gave Bahia the right to play Copa Libertadores for a third time. It was a real shock for the southern press because Salvador is in the Northeast, the poorest region of Brazil, and the victory was over Internacional, a team from southern Brazil, the region that has the highest Human Development Index of the country.

Dark years

In 1996, Bahia needed to win the last game of the season, but the club was relegated to Série B for the first time in its history after a 0–0 draw against Juventude at the Fonte Nova stadium. In 1999, Bahia was close to being promoted to Série A again. Bahia had a very good season, but finished in 3rd place, which was not enough to see them promoted. In order to be promoted, Bahia would have to win the final match against Brasiliense, but the referee Paulo César de Oliveira was assigned to that match, and many people say he was all but fair on that day.

In 2000, due to bribe scandals involving clubs such as São Paulo F.C. and Internacional, the team returned to the Brazilian First Division, invited by the Clube dos Treze, along with Fluminense, which was made a scapegoat for the controversy and was nationally victimized by the media (see Copa João Havelange).

In 2002, the bank that had fully sponsored the team went bankrupt, and Bahia began a descent down the Brazilian football pyramid. After the title of the Northeast Cup in 2001 and 2002, Bahia had a horrible year in 2003, and was relegated to the Série B for the second time in the club's history. In 2004, the team was close to getting promoted to the Série A again, finishing 4th. In 2005, the club again competed in the Série B, finishing in 18th place, and was relegated to the Série C for the first time in the club's history.

Fênix tricolor (tricolored phoenix)

Bahia finished 2007 amongst the first four teams of the Third Division's octagon, and were promoted to the Second Division for the 2008 season, but it was not easy. Bahia began strongly, but the last game of the 3rd stage of the Série C against the already-eliminated Fast Club was one of the most difficult games in the club's history. Bahia needed to win to advance to the final octagon. The victory came in the very last minute of the game, with a goal scored by Charles. During the final octagon, the team finished the third division in 2nd place, only losing the title in the final round.[citation needed]

This moment is called the "Fênix Tricolor" amongst Bahia fans.[citation needed] The phoenix represents Bahia re-surging from the ashes.

Despite playing in the Third Division of Brazilian football in 2007, Bahia had the largest average attendance in Brazil: 40,400 people per match.[citation needed] No club in the Third, the Second, or even the First Division was able to match it.[citation needed] However, this is not unusual for Bahia; having also achieved the biggest average attendance in Brazil in 2004 (Second Division), 1988 (First Division), 1986 (First Division), and 1985 (First Division).[citation needed]

Symbols

Bahia's colors are blue, red, and white. The blue color is a homage to Associação Atlética da Bahia; white, to Clube Baiano de Tênis; and red is a color present in the Bahia state flag. The club's mascot is called *Super-Homem Tricolor*, meaning Tricolour Superman, inspired by the DC Comics character. The mascot was created by the famous cartoonist Ziraldo based on the expression "*Esquadrão de Aço*" (*Steel Squad* in English), and wears a costume very similar to the original Superman's costume, which shares the team's colors.

Titles

Only senior titles are listed below.

- **National:**
  - *Campeonato Brasileiro:* 1988
  - *Taça Brasil:* 1959
- **Regional:**
  - *Northeast Cup:* 2 times (2001, 2002)
  - *North-Northeast Cup:* 4 times (1948, 1959, 1961, 1963)
- **State:**
  - *Bahia State League:* 43 times (1931, 1933, 1934, 1936, 1938 [1], 1940, 1944, 1945, 1947, 1948, 1949, 1950, 1952, 1954, 1956, 1958, 1959, 1960, 1961, 1962, 1967, 1970, 1971, 1973, 1974, 1975, 1976, 1977, 1978, 1979, 1981, 1982, 1983, 1984, 1986, 1987, 1988, 1991, 1993, 1994, 1998, 1999 [2], 2001)
    - *Runner-up:* 9 times (1941, 1964, 1972, 1989, 1997, 2000, 2004, 2005 and 2007)
  - *Bahia's State Trophy:* 3 times (2000, 2002, 2007)
    - *Runner-up:* 2 times (2004, 2006)
  - *Begin's Tournament:* 9 times (1931, 1932, 1934, 1937, 1938, 1951, 1964, 1967, 1979)
- **Other Titles**
  - *Relâmpago Tournament:* 2 times (1939, 1940)
  - *Quadrangular Tournament:* 2 times (1950, 1962)
  - *Octávio Mangabeira Tournament (Fonte Nova inauguration):* 1951
  - Bernardo Martins Catharino Trophy: 3 times (1953, 1954, 1955)
  - Vivaldo Tavares Trophy: 1955
  - *Friendship Tournament (Uruguay):* 1959
  - *Walter Passos Trophy:* 1962
  - *Bahia-Pernambuco Tournament:* 2 times (1993, 1994)
  - *International Renner Cup:* 1997
  - *Maria Quitéria Tournament:* 1998

Notable players

Esporte Clube Bahia

- José Sanfilippo
- Alencar
- Baiaco
- Beijoca
- Bobô
- Carlito
- Charles
- Charles Fabian
- Cícero Santos (still active, plays for Hertha Berlin in Germany)
- Cláudio Adão
- Daniel Alves (still active, plays for FC Barcelona in Spain)
- Douglas
- Eliseu
- Jorge Wagner (still active, plays for Sao Paulo FC)
- Luiz Henrique
- Mailson
- Mário
- Marito
- Naldinho
- Sandro
- Roberto Rebouças
- Serginho (former player of AC Milan in Italy)
- William Andem
- Rodolfo Rodríguez

Current squad

First Team

Note: Flags indicate national team as has been defined under FIFA eligibility rules. Players may hold more than one non-FIFA nationality.

No.	Position	Player
—	GK	Fernando
—	GK	Renê
—	GK	Omar
—	DF	Arílton *(on load Internacional)*
—	DF	Ávine
—	DF	Diego
—	DF	Nen
—	DF	Alison
—	DF	Vágner
—	DF	Diego
—	MF	Marcone
—	MF	Fábio Bahia *(on load Goiás)*
—	MF	Bruno Octávio *(on load Corinthians)*

No.	Position	Player
—	MF	Hélder
—	MF	Leandro
—	MF	Ananias
—	MF	Vander
—	MF	Felipe
—	MF	Morais *(on load Corinthians)*
—	MF	Rogerinho
—	FW	Adriano
—	FW	Aleílson
—	FW	Itacaré *(on load Vitória)*
—	FW	Jael
—	FW	Mendes
—	FW	Rodrigo Gral

Out on loan

Note: Flags indicate national team as has been defined under FIFA eligibility rules. Players may hold more than one non-FIFA nationality.

No.	Position	Player
—	FW	Mário *(at Confiança)*

Stadium

Games were played in Fonte Nova stadium until the disaster occurred in November 2007. At the game against Vila Nova (a game of Bahia's promotion), part of the stadium collapsed and 7 people died. More than 30 were injured. After that episode, the government of the state declared that the stadium would be demolished. Bahia had always played at the Fonte Nova stadium, since its inauguration in 1951. Some notable games at the Fonte Nova:

- Bahia–Internacional 2–1 (Série A – Final – 1988)
- Bahia–Fluminense 2–1 (Série A – Semi-Final – 1988)
- Bahia–Flamengo 4–1 (Série A – 2001)

- Bahia–Sport Recife 3–1 (Northeast Cup – Final – 2002)
- Bahia–Fast Club 1–0 (Série C – 3rd Stage – 2007)

Bahia's state championship games are now played at the Pituaçu Stadium, which has a capacity of 32,157 spectators.

External links

- Official Site [1] (www.esporteclubebahia.com.br)
- Web Store [2] (www.lojadobahia.com.br)
- Supporter Advantages [3] (www.borabahea.com.br)
- Supporter Advantages (More expensive) [4] (http://www.nocoracaodobahia.com.br/)
- Unofficial Site [5] (www.ecbahia.com.br)

Galícia Esporte Clube

Full name	Galícia Esporte Clube
Nickname(s)	*Azulino (Blue One)* *Granadeiro (Grenadier)* *Demolidor de Campeões (Champions Crusher)*
Founded	1933
Ground	Parque Santiago, Salvador, Brazil (Capacity: 8,000)
Chairman	Raimundo Nonato Reis
Manager	-
League	-
2006	-

| Home colours | Away colours |

Galícia Esporte Clube is a Brazilian football club from Salvador, capital of the state of Bahia, in Brazil's northeast region.

Galícia's chairmain (2007) is Raimundo Nonato Reis.

History

Galícia was founded on January 1, 1933 by immigrants from the autonomous region of Galicia, Spain. Its founder and first president was Mr. Eduardo Castro de la Iglesias.

Galícia was the first club to win the Bahia League Championship (Campeonato Baiano) three times in a row, quickly becoming one of the strongest teams in the state. In its first decade, the club won the League in 1937, 1941, 1942 and 1943, being runner-up another five times (1935, 1936, 1938, 1939 and 1940).

However, after this superb beginning, the club only managed to return to the top in 1968, with its fifth and last Bahia League title. Besides, it was runner-up in 1967, 1980, 1982 and 1995.

Galícia's best regional performance was in 1969, when it was runner-up of the Northeast Zone of the North-Northeast Cup (Copa Norte-Nordeste). The club only played twice in the Brazilian League (Campeonato Brasileiro) First Division: 1981 and 1983.

In 1999, the team was relegated to Bahia League's Second Division.

In 2001, Galícia occupied 54th place in the Brazilian Football Clubs Ranking of the prestigious "Placar" magazine.

Stadiums

Main articles: Estádio Parque Santiago, Estádio Fonte Nova, and Estádio de Pituaçu

In its early years, Galícia played in the old "Campo da Graça" stadium. After its demolition, its home matches moved to Salvador's biggest stadium, Fonte Nova, and sometimes to Pituaçu Stadium. Nowadays, the club has its own stadium, the Parque Santiago, with a seating capacity of 8,000 fans.

Symbols

Galícia's nicknames are "Demolidor de Campeões" ("Champions' Demolisher"), "Azulino" ("The Blue One") and "Granadeiro" ("grenadier").

Galícia's logo is white, with a blue diagonal strip featuring the letters "G", "E" and "C", and a Saint James Cross in the center, remembering its galicean heritage. The players wear blue shirts and white shorts and socks. The club anthem was composed by Francisco Icó da Silva.

Titles

Bahia League Championship (Campeonato Baiano)

Champion

- 1937
- 1941
- 1942
- 1943
- 1968

Runner-up

- 1935
- 1936
- 1938
- 1939
- 1940
- 1967
- 1980
- 1982
- 1995

Bahia League Championship Second Level (Campeonato Baiano Segunda Divisão)

Champion

- 1985
- 1988

Runner-up

- 2007

Northeast Zone of the North-Northeast Cup (Copa Norte-Nordeste)

Runner-up

- 1969

Idols

Some well-known Brazilian players started their careers in Galícia, like the defender Toninho and the center-forwards Washington and Oséas, all of which played in Brazil's National Team. Another great player who defended Galícia was Marinho Peres, Brazilian champion in 1976 with Internacional and defender of the "Seleção" in Germany World Cup - 1974.

One of Galícia's most remarkable coaches was Aymoré Moreira, who led Brazil to its second World Championship in Chile-1962. With Mr. Moreira, Galícia was runner-up in the Bahia League in 1980.

External links

- GALÍCIA ESPORTE CLUBE - Official Site [1]
- Granadeiros Azulinos - Galícia Esporte Clube (Non-official site) [2]
- Galícia EC's Anthem [3]
- Brazilian Football Statistics at RSSSF [4]
- Bahia State League List of Champions at RSSSF [5]

Associação Desportiva Leônico

Full name	Associação Desportiva Leônico
Founded	April 3, 1940
Ground	Edgard Santos (Capacity: 5,000)
League	-

Home colours   Away colours

Associação Desportiva Leônico, commonly known as **Leônico**, are a Brazilian football team from Salvador. They won the Campeonato Baiano once and competed in the Série A two times.

History

They were founded on April 3, 1940. Leônico won the Campeonato Baiano in 1966. The club competed in the Série A in 1979 and in 1985.

Stadium

They play their home games at the Edgard Santos stadium, located in Simões Filho. The stadium has a maximum capacity of 5,000 people. They played in the 1990s at Estádio José Trindade Lobo, a stadium located in Santo Antônio de Jesus. This stadium has a maximum capacity of 4,000 people.

Achievements

- **Campeonato Baiano:**
  - **Winners (1):** 1966

Esporte Clube Vitória

Full name	Esporte Clube Vitória
Nickname(s)	*Leão da Barra* ("Lion from Barra")
Founded	1899
Ground	Barradão, Salvador, Brazil (Capacity: 35,632)
Chairman	Alexi Portela
Manager	Antônio Lopes
League	Campeonato Brasileiro Série A
2009	Campeonato Brasileiro Série A, 13th

Home colours	Away colours	Third colours

Esporte Clube Vitória, usually known simply as **Vitória**, is a Brazilian football team from Salvador in Bahia, founded on May 13, 1899.

Vitória's home games are played at the club's own stadium (Manoel Barradas, capacity 35,632). They play in red and black horizontal striped shirts, black shorts and black socks. The stripes have changed over time: they have been sometimes vertical, horizontal, wide and narrow.

History

The club was founded on May 13, 1899, by the brothers Artur and Artêmio Valente. They were from a traditional Bahian family and discovered football during their studies in England. Initially, however, Vitória was a cricket club named **Club de Cricket Victoria**.

On May 22, 1901, Vitória played its first football match, at Campo da Pólvora, against International Sport Club, a team whose players were English seamen. Vitória beat International 3-2. Two months after that match, Vitória changed its original colors, which were black and white, to red and black, which are still in use.

On September 13, 1903, Vitória beat Paulista settlement São Paulo-Bahia 2-0. This match was the club's first professional match.

In 1908, Vitória won its first title ever, the Campeonato Baiano.

In 1998, the **Vitória S/A** was founded (short for *Vitória Sociedade Anônima*), which is an incorporated company created to manage the club's professional football businesses.

In 2004, Vitória, after a poor campaign, was relegated to the Brazilian Second Division.

1908 Bahia State Champions - Milzen, Álvaro Tarquinio e Mario Pereira; A. C. Martins, Adriano Porto e Noé Nunes; Armando Gordilho, Oscar Alves, Fernando Alves, C. Muller, R. Mc. Nair, Oscar Luz, A. Galeão e Alfredo Seixas.

In 2005, the club competed in the Brazilian Second Division finishing 17th and so was relegated to the Third Division.

In 2006, Vitória was sub-champion of the Third Division, being promoted to the Brazilian Second Division.

In 2007, Vitória played the Brazilian Second Division and was promoted back to the Brazilian First Division after finishing in 4th place. This means the club managed to return from the lowest Brazilian division to its original place in the First Division in only two years.

Titles

Major competitions

- Campeonato do Nordeste: 1997, 1999, 2003
- 26 State Championships: 1908, 1909, 1953, 1955, 1957, 1964, 1965, 1972, 1980, 1985, 1989, 1990, 1992, 1995, 1996, 1997, 1999, 2000, 2002, 2003, 2004, 2005, 2007, 2008, 2009, 2010
- Brazil Cup: Runner-Up 2010
- Brazilian Championship: Runner-Up 1993
- Campeonato Brasileiro Série B: Runner-Up 1992
- Campeonato Brasileiro Série C: Runner-Up 2006

Other competitions
- Torneio Maria Quitéria: 1996

Youth competitions
- Dallas Cup: 1996, 1997
- Taça Belo Horizonte de Juniores: 1994
- Milk Cup: 1999
- Phillips/Otten Cup: 1995, 1996, 1997, 2004, 2005, 2006
- USA Cup: 1997, 1998
- Rotary Cup: 1997, 1998
- Sparkasen Cup: 1996, 1997
- Austria Cup: 1999
- Bayer Cup: 1997, 1999
- Riviera Cup: 1999
- Nike Premier Cup: 2001

Current squad

First team

Note: Flags indicate national team as has been defined under FIFA eligibility rules. Players may hold more than one non-FIFA nationality.

No.	Position	Player
—	GK	Julián Viáfara
—	GK	Renan Rocha
—	GK	Gustavo
—	GK	Lee
—	DF	Léo
—	DF	Jonas
—	DF	Nino
—	DF	Wallace
—	DF	Anderson Martins
—	DF	Reniê
—	DF	Egídio *(on loan from Flamengo)*
—	MF	Vanderson

No.	Position	Player
—	MF	Marconi
—	MF	Uelliton
—	MF	Ricardo Conceição
—	MF	Bida
—	MF	Neto

No.	Position	Player
—	MF	Ramon Menezes
—	MF	Arthur Maia
—	MF	Elkeson
—	MF	Kleiton Domingues
—	MF	Fernando
—	MF	Thiago Humberto *(on loan from Internacional)*
—	FW	Renato
—	FW	Adaílton
18	FW	Schwenck
—	FW	Júnior
—	FW	Edson
—	FW	Marcos Bambam
—	FW	Jacson
—	FW	Soares
—	FW	Henrique *(on loan from São Paulo)*

Out on loan

Note: Flags indicate national team as has been defined under FIFA eligibility rules. Players may hold more than one non-FIFA nationality.

No.	Position	Player
--	FW	Neto Baiano *(on loan to JEF United until 2011)*
--	FW	Índio *(on loan to Chunnam Dragons until 2011)*

Mascot

The club's mascot is a lion named Lelê Leão (Lion), and according to Vitória's official site, his objective is to stimulate the club's supporters and players on match days.

Competitions record

The competitions record of Vitória's last ten seasons:

- Champion.
- Runner-up.
- Promoted.
- Relegated.

Year	Campeonato Baiano					Campeonato Brasileiro							Copa do Brasil					Copa do Nordeste					Copa Sudamericana				
	Pos	G	W	D	L	Division	Pos	G	W	D	L	Pos	G	W	D	L	Pos	G	W	D	L	Pos	G	W	D	L
2001	4°	10	5	1	4	Série A	16°	27	9	9	9	14°	6	3	1	2	7°	15	6	3	6	-	-	-	-	-
2002	1°	12	7	3	2	Série A	10°	25	11	4	10	25°	4	1	2	1	2°	19	12	3	4	-	-	-	-	-
2003	1°	14	9	2	3	Série A	16°	46	15	11	20	7°	8	4	0	4	1°	5	3	2	0	-	-	-	-	-
2004	1°	14	10	3	1	Série A	23°	46	13	9	24	4°	10	5	1	4	-	-	-	-	-	-	-	-	-	-
2005	1°	14	9	5	0	Série B	17°	21	7	6	8	23°	4	1	0	3	-	-	-	-	-	-	-	-	-	-
2006	2°	34	21	8	5	Série C	2°	32	18	5	9	9°	6	3	2	1	-	-	-	-	-	-	-	-	-	-
2007	1°	28	20	6	2	Série B	4°	38	18	5	15	26°	4	1	2	1	-	-	-	-	-	-	-	-	-	-
2008	1°	28	16	4	8	Série A	10°	38	15	7	16	26°	3	2	0	1	-	-	-	-	-	-	-	-	-	-
2009	1°	26	19	3	4	Série A	13°	38	13	9	16	8°	8	2	4	2	-	-	-	-	-	14°	4	1	1	2
2010	1°	22	14	4	4	Série A	-	-	-	-	-	-	-	-	-	-	-	-	-	-	-	-	-	-	-	-

Notable former players

- Bebeto
- David Luiz
- Dida
- Dudu Cearense
- Edílson
- Obina
- Ramon
- Túlio Maravilha
- Vampeta
- Víctor Aristizábal
- Dejan Petkovic

Notable coaches

- Toninho Cerezo
- Péricles Chamusca
- Paulo César Carpegiani
- Aymoré Moreira
- Carlos Volante
- Carlos Castilho
- Orlando Peçanha de Carvalho

Ultras

- Camisa 12 [1]
- Os Imbatíveis [2] - Founded in 1997, is one of the most active ultras in Brazil.

External links

- Official Site [3]
- Leaodabarra.com [4]

Esporte Clube Ypiranga

Full name	Esporte Clube Ypiranga
Founded	7 September 1906
Ground	Vila Canária (Capacity: 4,000)
President	Valdemar Filho
Head coach	Fabio marques

The **Esporte Clube Ypiranga** is a football team with headquarters in Salvador, Brasil's Northeast Region. Its colours are yellow and black.

It is the third team in Bahia with more titles in the Baiano Championship, coming after Bahia and Vitória, with 10 titles.

History

Ypiranga was founded in 7 September 1906; it is one of the oldest football team in Bahia.

In the beginning of the 20th century, young men excluded from society for various reason, mainly social and economic, founded **Sport Club Sete de Setembro**, in 17 April 1904, in 7 September 1906 the team was closed down, but a new team called **Sport Club Ypiranga** (nowadays called **Esporte Clube Ypiranga**) was founded.

The Esporte Clube Ypiranga is the union of the poor people of the city, who want to break the tradition of the fortunates to continue the exploitation of the poor and last fortunates.

Ypiranga isn't the team that only takes advantage of black and poor players who are part of its team, It was founded and directed by this layer of society, most of its supporters were socially excluded too. "Other football teams from Bahia can be wealthy, more prosperous, more hunted by the media, even have a higher number of supporters. Though none had a tradition so glorious as E.C. Ypiranga. This is the team of the World Box Champion Acelino de Freitas and of our beloved Jorge Amado, it used to be powerful, wealthy, invincible, Superchampion... The Ypiranga may have lost its excitement, because it has already experienced many victories, it has made its supporters very happy. If a visitor has to chose a football team, may it be Ypiranga.

Now, the team is playing the 2nd division of Campeonato Baiano.

Nowadays

The team did not play in the 2nd dividion in 2008. the current situation is that the team is going through a very difficult financial crises, the lack of resources is so dreadful that the under 18 team faced huge challenges during the campeonato baiano de juniores.

In the current moment there is an honest group which works with all power and possible tools to relive as a phoenix. They hope to be back in 2010 for the campeonato baiano de futebol.

Below is the newest administrative team of the dearest Ypiranga

New leadership: Valdemar Filho - President. Fabio Marques - Marketing and communication director. Paulo Mauricio - Planning and control director. Rafael Mendes - football director. Ramon Brito - solicitor. Victor Novaes - Web Designer. Priscylla Watson - International relation. Naama Rodrigues - advertising and marketing officer. Bruno Oliveira - Marketing Assistant. Edvan de Barros - System Analyst. Jomar Negreiros - System Analys. Ivana Carolina - Social assistant. Emerson Ferretti - Manager

Achievements

Regional

- **Copa Norte-Nordeste:** 1951.

Statehood

- **Campeonato Baiano:** 10 times (1917, 1918, 1920, 1921, 1925, 1928, 1929, 1932, 1939 and 1951).
- Vice-Campeonato Baiano: 10 times (1915, 1924, 1926, 1927, 1931, 1933, 1937, 1938, 1946 and 1949).
- **Campeonato Baiano Second Level:** 2 times (1983 e 1990*).
- Vice-Campeonato Baiano Second Level runners-up: 1989.
- **Torneio Início**: 8 times (1919, 1922, 1929, 1933, 1947, 1956, 1959 e 1963).
- Torneio Início runners-up: 10 times (1915, 1924, 1926, 1927, 1931, 1933, 1937, 1938, 1942 and 1949).

* being a invictus champion.

This is a translation of the page Esporte Clube Ypiranga in Portuguese into the English language click to go the page in Portuguese.

ATP Itaparica

Sul America Open Citibank Open	
Defunct tennis tournament	
Created	1986
Ended	1990
Event name	Sul America Open (1986-1987) Citibank Open (1988-1990)
Location	Itaparica, Brazil (1986–1990)
Tour	ATP Tour (1990) Grand Prix circuit (1986–89)
Surface	Hard (1986–1990)

Known by various names, this is a defunct men's tennis tournament that was part of the Grand Prix tennis circuit from 1986 to 1989 and the ATP Tour in 1990. The event was held in Itaparica, Brazil and was played on outdoor hard courts.

One Brazilian reached the final, Luiz Mattar in 1986, when he was beaten by Andre Agassi. It was Agassi's first win on the main ATP Tour. In 1990, Mats Wilander won his final career tournament here.

Results

Singles

Year	Name of Tournament	Champion	Runner-up	Score
1986	Sul America Open	Andrés Gómez	Jean-Philippe Fleurian	4–6, 6–4, 6–4
1987	Sul America Open	Andre Agassi	Luiz Mattar	7–6, 6–2
1988	Citibank Open	Jaime Yzaga	Javier Frana	7–6, 6–2
1989	Citibank Open	Martín Jaite	Jay Berger	6–4, 6–4
1990	Citibank Open	Mats Wilander	Marcelo Filippini	6–1, 6–2

Doubles

Year	Champion	Runner-up	Score
1986	Chip Hooper Mike Leach	Loïc Courteau Guy Forget	7–5, 6–3
1987	Sergio Casal Emilio Sánchez	Jorge Lozano Diego Pérez	6–2, 6–2
1988	Sergio Casal Emilio Sánchez	Jorge Lozano Todd Witsken	7–6, 7–6
1989	Rick Leach Jim Pugh	Jorge Lozano Todd Witsken	6–2, 7–6
1990	Mauro Menezes Fernando Roese	Tomás Carbonell Marcos-Aurelio Gorriz-Bonhora	7–6, 7–5

References

- ATP Tour website [1]

Estádio Parque Santiago

Estádio Parque Santiago is a multi-use stadium located in Salvador, Brazil. It is used mostly for football matches and hosts the home matches of Galícia Esporte Clube. The stadium has a maximum capacity of 8,000 people.

The stadium was built with the help of the Spanish community of Salvador.

External links

- Estádio Parque Santiago [1]

Geographical coordinates: 12°59′00″S 38°28′23″W

Estádio de Pituaçu

Estádio de Pituaçu	
Location	Salvador, Brazil
Opened	1979
Owner	Bahia State Government
Surface	Grass
Capacity	32,157
Field dimensions	110 x 68m
Tenants	
Esporte Clube Bahia	

Estádio Metropolitano Roberto Santos, usually known as **Estádio de Pituaçu**, is a football stadium located in Salvador, Bahia state, Brazil. The stadium is owned by the Government of Bahia state and it was built in 1979. Its formal name honors Roberto Santos, who was a federal deputy, the governor of Bahia state from 1975 to 1979, a professor at the Universidade Federal da Bahia's Faculty of Medicine, and was the Minister of Health during José Sarney's government. The stadium became one of the most important stadiums in Bahia after the Fonte Nova stadium's demolition was announced, and it has a maximum capacity of 32,157 people, but it will be expanded to a maximum capacity of 34,000 people.

History

The stadium construction concluded in 1979. The inaugural match was played on March 11 of that year, when Bahia beat Fluminense de Feira 2-0. The first goal of the stadium was scored by Bahia's Douglas.

The stadium's attendance record currently stands at 18,418, set on April 2, 1995, when Vitória beat Bahia 2-0.

On January 21, 2008, the stadium reformation started. It was planned to be concluded in August of the same year, but it was delayed to October due to a workers' strike. Its maximum capacity will be expanded to 34,000 people, and it will be adapted to be in accordance with the Brazilian Supporters' Statute (Estatuto do Torcedor).

Estádio de Pituaçu hosted the 2010 World Cup Qualifying game between Brazil and Chile, played on September 9, 2009, and won by the Brazilians 4-2.

References

Geographical coordinates: 12°56'47.89"S 38°25'1.27"W

Estádio Fonte Nova

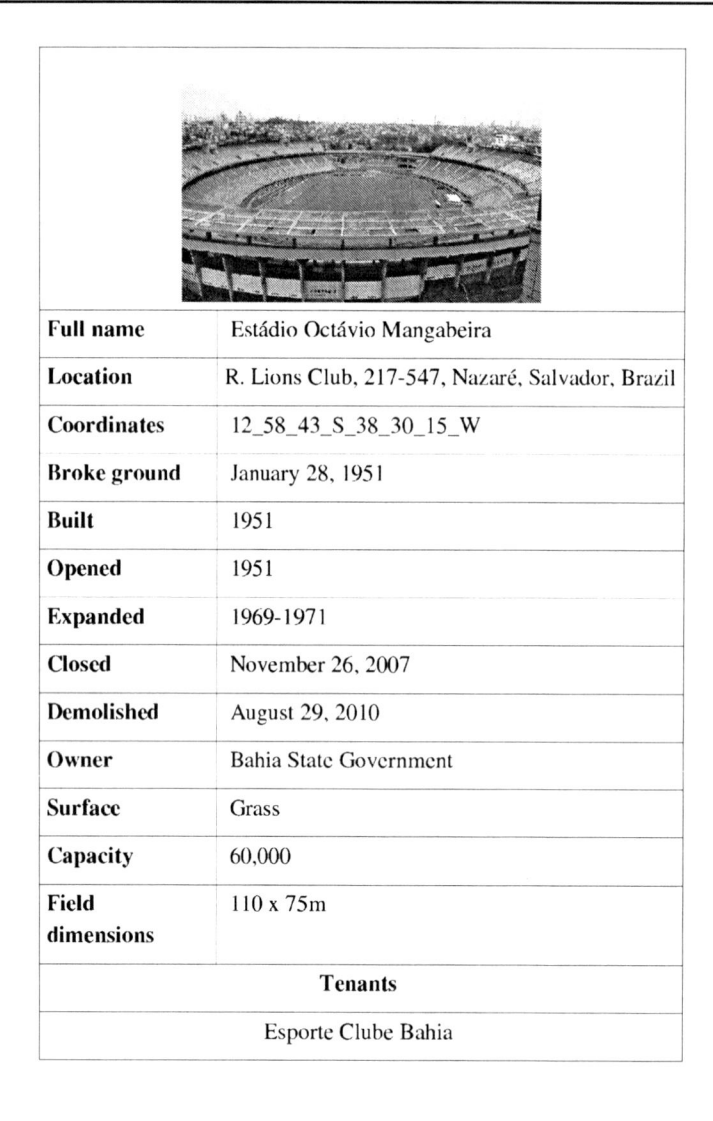

Full name	Estádio Octávio Mangabeira
Location	R. Lions Club, 217-547, Nazaré, Salvador, Brazil
Coordinates	12_58_43_S_38_30_15_W
Broke ground	January 28, 1951
Built	1951
Opened	1951
Expanded	1969-1971
Closed	November 26, 2007
Demolished	August 29, 2010
Owner	Bahia State Government
Surface	Grass
Capacity	60,000
Field dimensions	110 x 75m
Tenants	
Esporte Clube Bahia	

The **Estádio Fonte Nova**, also known as **Estádio Octávio Mangabeira**, was a football stadium inaugurated on January 28, 1951 in Salvador, Bahia, with a maximum capacity of 66,080 people. The stadium was owned by the Bahia government, and was the home ground of Esporte Clube Bahia. Its formal name honors Octávio Cavalcanti Mangabeira, a civil engineer, journalist, and former Bahia state governor from 1947 to 1954.

Estádio Fonte Nova.

After part of the upper terraces collapsed, killing 7 people and injuring several others, the government of Bahia announced the demolition of Fonte Nova and the construction of a new stadium, the Arena da Bahia, in the same place.

The stadium was nicknamed Fonte Nova because it was located at Ladeira das Fontes das Pedras.

History

The stadium construction ended in 1951. On March 4, 1971, the stadium was reinaugurated, after a great reformation involving the addition of a second tier, which expanded the maximum stadium capacity from 35,000 to 110,000. In the reinauguration day, two matches were played: Bahia against Flamengo, and Vitória against Grêmio. On that day happened a big tumult, where two people died.

The inaugural match was played on January 28, 1951, when Guarany and Botafogo, both local Bahia state teams, drew 2-1. The first goal of the stadium was scored by Guarany's Nélson.

The stadium's attendance record currently stands at 110,438, set on February 12, 1989 when **Bahia beat Fluminense 2-1**.

On November 25, 2007, when the Brazilian Championship Third Division match between Bahia and Vila Nova was nearly over with more than 60,000 supporters in attendance, a section of the stadium's highest terraces collapsed when Bahia's supporters were celebrating the club's promotion to the Brazilian Championship Second Division, killing seven people and injuring forty others. Jacques Wagner, who is the governor of Bahia state, ordered the stadium to be closed as the causes of the accident are under investigation by the authorities, and he also said on November 26, 2007 that the stadium may be demolished if its structure is compromised. On November 27, 2007, the governor of Bahia announced that Estádio Fonte Nova will be demolished, and a new stadium will be built in its place. On September 28, 2008, Bahia's governor Jaques Wagner announced that instead of being demolished, the stadium will be reformed into a multiuse arena with a maximum capacity of 60,000 people seated.

Demolition of the Octavio Mangabeira Stadium began in June 2010 and is expected to be finished by August - the upper tier was demolished using explosives on the 30th of August 2010. After the implosion, a portion of the upper tier was left standing, which is currently being dismantled manually. The Bahia Arena will be constructed on its former site.

A new stadium in the city is being constructed as a venue for the 2016 Summer Olympics for football tournaments.

External links

- Estádio Fonte Nova at World Stadiums [1]

Geographical coordinates: 12°58′43.7″S 38°30′15.1″W

Barradão

Full name	Estádio Manoel Barradas
Location	Salvador, Bahia, Brazil
Owner	Vitória
Operator	Vitória
Capacity	35,632
Tenants	
Vitória	

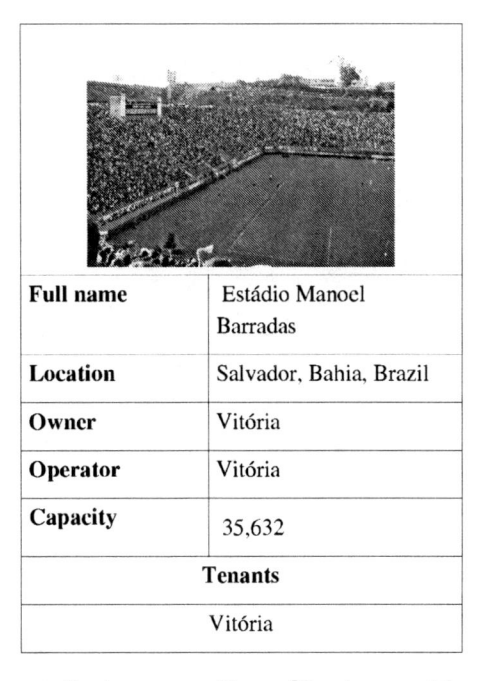

Estádio Manoel Barradas, usually known as **Barradão**, is a multi-purpose stadium in Salvador, Brazil. It is currently used mostly for football matches. The stadium has a current maximum capacity of 35,632 people. The stadium was built in 1986 and reinaugurated in 1991.

The Barradão is owned by Esporte Clube Vitória. The stadium is named after Manoel Barradas, who was a Vitória's counselor.

History

In 1986, the works on Barradão were completed. The inaugural match was played on November 9 of that year, when Vitória and Santos drew 1-1. The first goal of the stadium was scored by Santos' Dino.

In 1991, the stadium was reformed. The reinaugural match was played on August 25 of that year, when Vitória and Olimpia of Paraguay drew 1-1. The first goal of the stadium after the reinauguration was scored by Olimpia's Jorge Campos.

The stadium's attendance record currently stands at 51,756, set in 1999 when Vitória beat Atlético Mineiro 2-1.

References

- *Enciclopédia do Futebol Brasileiro*, Volume 2 - Lance, Rio de Janeiro: Aretê Editorial S/A, 2001.

External links

- www.fussballtempel.net [1]

Geographical coordinates: 12°55′08″S 38°25′37″W

Cities Nearby with Attractions

Porto Seguro

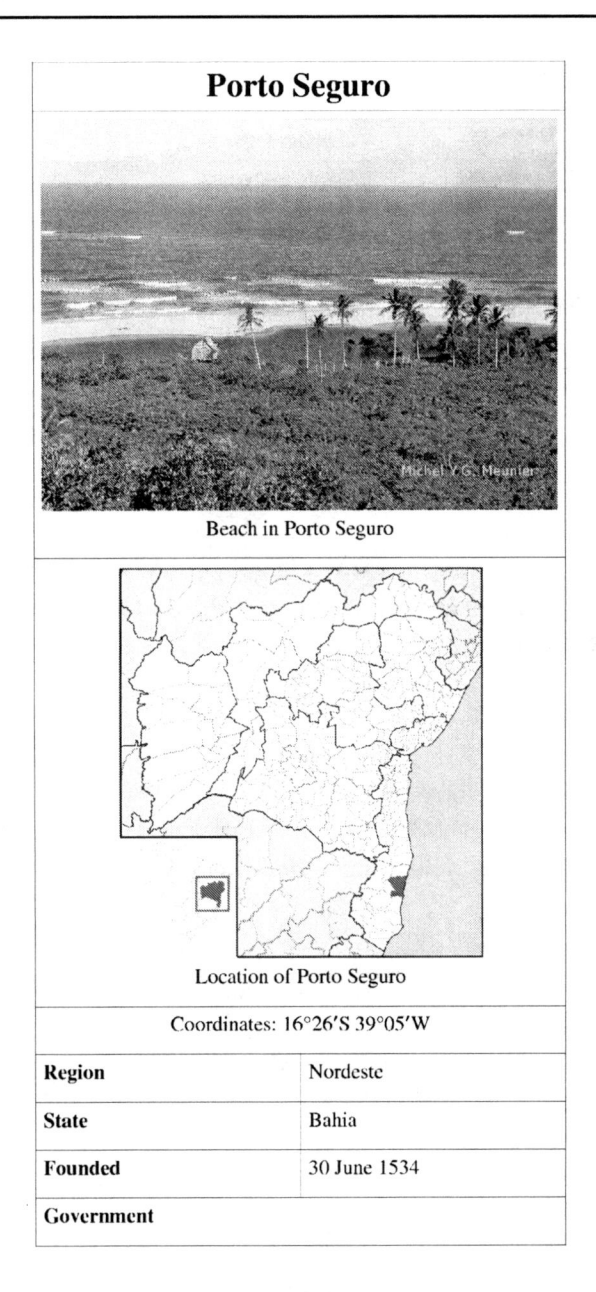

Porto Seguro	
Beach in Porto Seguro	
Location of Porto Seguro	
Coordinates: 16°26′S 39°05′W	
Region	Nordeste
State	Bahia
Founded	30 June 1534
Government	

- Mayor	Gilberto Abade (PSB)
Area	
- Total	2.408 km² (0.9 sq mi)
Elevation	4 m (13 ft)
Population (2006)	
- Total	140,000
- Density	58/km² (150.2/sq mi)
Time zone	UTC-3
Postal code	45810-000
Website	[1]

Porto Seguro is a municipality in the Brazilian state of Bahia. It is the site where the Portuguese explorer Pedro Álvares Cabral first set foot on Brazilian soil on April 22, 1500. It was the busiest port of the developing Portuguese colonies from 1500 into the early 19th century and is now a major tourist destination.

Location

Porto Seguro is located on the Atlantic coast at a midway point between Salvador and Vitória. It is 707 km. south of Salvador and 613 km. north of Vitória. It is 62 km. east of the connection with the important BR-101 highway at Eunápolis.

Airport

The Porto Seguro Airport was completed in 1993, and it receives direct flights from Salvador, São Paulo, Belo Horizonte, Porto Alegre, Curitiba and Rio de Janeiro. The airlines serving the city are Varig, Tam, Gol, and Ocean Air, besides the charters flights arriving from Europe: Portugal, the Netherlands, Italy and France.

Tourism

The region is also notable for its many beaches and vestiges of its colonial past. There are still vestiges of the Atlantic Tropical Forest nearby. There are also a number of beach-side dance floors, playing Bahia's popular music, known as "Axé".

Tourism has expanded fast in recent years and there is highly visible growth in Porto Seguro. What was once a small town of fewer than 10,000 people in the 1970s has become a city of over 100,000 people. One suburb on the southern bank of the Buranhém River, Arraial d'Ajuda, has grown from approximately 900 people in 1990 to 11,411 in 2005.

Carnival

The city offers one of the most famous Carnival parties in Bahia. "Electric Trios" (trucks carrying sound systems and live bands), dancing "blocos" and "cordões" (street dancing groups) drag thousands of tourists along the "Passarela do Álcool" Passageway (the traditional local avenue) and to beach bars.

Economic information

The economy is based on services, tourism, light transformation industries, fishing, government employment, agriculture, and cattle raising.

In 2003 there were 66,513 head of cattle, of which 8,647 were milk cows. The main agricultural products were pineapple, sugarcane, manioc, banana, rubber (19.8 km² in 2003), cacau (6.4 km²), coffee, coconut (19.95 km²), guava, oranges, lemons, papaya (10 km²), passion fruit, and pepper.

Attractions

Night Leisure The Passarela do Álcool Passageway is a famous spot in the city. Here, visitors find the famous "Capeta" drink, can have dinner with live music and buy gifts made in the region; or visitors may go to Capitania dos Peixes, on Pacu Island, with ecological landscapes and an assorted variety of music genres and ambiences, near giant aquariums.

Historical Downtown Area The historical site in the Cidade Alta area is a National Heritage Monument put under government trust by a Federal Decree since 1973. It was one of the first towns in Brazil and played an important role during the first years of European colonization. It includes three churches and around 40 buildings (among private residential houses and public institutions), restored by the State Government for the 500th anniversary celebration of Brazilian "discovery". At night the whole area is bathed by a special lighting system, offering an impressive view.

Monte Pascoal National Park Created in 1961 to preserve the place where Brazil was "discovered" by Portuguese warriors. It includes swamp areas, salt marshes, river marshes and a coastline around the rocky, high and round hill, considered the first point of land to be seen by the Portuguese traveler Pedro

Álvares Cabral's crew. It extends over an area of 144.8 km², including the Pataxó tribe's indigenous protection land. Besides its historical importance, it also offers protection to one of the last stretches of Atlantic forest in the Northeastern area of Brazil. The area is aimed at preserving valuable woods such as Brazil wood, and still hosts many species of animals threatened by extinction, such as "collar sloth", "black burs", among others.

Recife de Fora Sea Park It was the first city owned park in Brazil. During low tide, visitor can view a wide range of coral reefs, fish and many sea species. Tours are available on schooners.

Glória Hillock Here, visitors find the ruins of what many consider to be the São Francisco Church, the where Ynaiá was buried, an Indian woman who died for the love of a crewmember of Portuguese navigator Gonçalo Coelho's fleet. People say the São Francisco Church was the first one built in Brazil, in baroque style, probably in 1504, whose ruins date to 1730.

The Nossa Senhora da Penha Matrix Church Located on Pero de Campos Tourinho Square, in Cidade Alta, it was built at the 18th century's end. It comprises an aisle, a main chapel, a sacristy and a bell tower.

Jaqueira Indigenous Protection Reservation A huge jackfruit tree trunk, tumbled down by nature itself, represents the return to one's origins and acts as a historical and cultural reference to honor the ancestral fathers and mothers of Pataxó families who recently moved into this 8.27 km² Indian protection area. Their huts, spread around original Atlantic Forest woods, keeps original old formats, giving visitors the impression of being back 500 years in time to pre-Columbian Brazil.

Pirata Island It is considered as one of the most sophisticated aquarium complexes in South America]].[citation needed] Pirata Island is a thematic leisure center combining nightlife infrastructure and environmental and sea biodiversity protection, with giant aquariums. It is located on Pacuio Island, on Buranhém River and access is available exclusively by boat.

The "Discovery" Outdoors Museum An outdoors, natural museum, whose "art galleries" are its beaches, valleys and natural trails and whose "collection" is a set of geographical formations and traditional villages, disposed as art works in permanent exhibition, engraved in very ancient media, which are spread along the 130 km length of Bahia's historical southern coastline.

Terravista Golf Course The golf course, designed by architect Dan Blankenship, offers 18 holes and demanded US$ 4 million in investment to be built]].[citation needed] The project follows the most sophisticated and up to date trends in golf course building in the world today, as done in California, USA, and in Algarve, Portugal – all of which look very similar in terms of weather and geographical conditions, for all three golf courses are close to sea areas.

External links
- Site of Porto Seguro's City Hall [1] (Portuguese)
- Voz de Trancoso - Site Ambiental [2]
- [[Category:Populated coastal places in Bahia [3]]

Feira de Santana

Feira de Santana	
— Municipality —	
The Municipality of Feira de Santana	
Flag	Seal
Localization of the city	
Country	Brazil
Region	Northeast
State	Bahia
Government	
- Mayor	Tárcisio Pimenta (PFL)
Area	
- Total	1362.880 km^2 (526.2 sq mi)
Elevation	286 m (938 ft)
Population (2006)	
- Total	700,000
- Density	392.8/km^2 (1017.3/sq mi)
Time zone	UTC-3 (UTC-3)
Postal Code	44000-000
Area code(s)	+55 75
Website	Feira de Santana, Bahia [1]

Feira de Santana is a city in Bahia, Brazil. It is the second most important city in the state, with a population of 700,000 according to IBGE's estimate. It is located 115 km northwest of Salvador, Bahia's capital city. These cities are connected by BR-324, a four-lane divided highway. Feira de Santana's nickname is "a princesa do sertao" or "the backcountry's princess".

Feira de Santana takes is name in honor of two of its founders. In the 18th century, Domingos Barbosa de Araujo and his wife Anna Brandoa built a chapel on the Fazenda Sant'Anna dos Olhos D'Água (*Saint Anna of the Fountains Plantation*). They dedicated the chapel to their Saint, Saint Anna. The city is also known as "The Gateway to the Backcountry", for its location in the Agreste zone, a geographic region that separates the wet "Zona da Mata" from the arid and desert "Sertão";

The location gradually became a common stopping point for voyagers and traders from the high "sertão" of Bahia and from other states on the trail to the port of Cachoeira and other important villages of Bahia. The area also developed a periodic market together with a prosperous cattle commerce.

Eventually many Brazilians and foreigners began to adopt the area that would become Feira de Santanta as their home. The City began to develop with wide streets which were bordered by many commercial houses serving the area's growing population. As the area's growth accelerated, the residents created the City of Feira de Santana. Feira de Santana became the second City in Bahia and the 31st City of Brazil. Feira de Santana's important geographic location and the hospitality of its people continued to attract new residents.

Today, Feira de Santana is the second largest City in Bahia. Feira de Santana also remains an important stopping point for travelers, containing a major junction of Northeastern Brazil's highways. The City functions as a crossroads for the traffic coming from the South and West-Central portions of Brazil and bound for Salvador and other important cities of the northeast. Feira de Santana, thanks in part to its longstanding importance as a crossroads and its proximity to Salvador, is an important and diverse commercial and industrial center. The Universidade Estadual de Feira de Santana is located in the city. The city is the seat of the Roman Catholic Archdiocese of Feira de Santana.

Feira de Santana is famous for its parties and festivals, such as Senhora Sant'Ana in the last week of July (26 July), which features activities such as bumba-meu-boi, segura-a-véia and burrinha. The Micareta carnival party is held 15 days after Passover; the Festival of Violeiros, in September; and the donkey race in November. The city boasts of several interesting tourist destinations including the market of popular arts, the museum of contemporary art and the Antares Astronomical Observatory.

See also: Largest Cities of Northeast Region, Brazil

Geographical coordinates: 12°15'S 38°57'W

Vitória da Conquista

Vitória da Conquista is a city in Bahia, Brazil which serves as a regional center for the smaller cities Barra do Choça, Planalto and Poções. These cities on the plateau, all around 1000 meters in elevation, form the basis of a strong traditional coffee-producing region as well as a rapidly-expanding center for new businesses.

It is the third largest city in the state of Bahia, after the state's capital, Salvador, and Feira de Santana. Its population, according to IBGE (Brazilian Institute of Geography and Statistics) registered 308,204 in April, 2007.

Vitória da Conquista, 2005

Climate

The climate is tropical and dry, moderated in temperature by the elevation. The altitude of the city itself varies between 857 meters (2811 feet) and 950 meters (3116 feet). Precipitation from April to August is often characterized by fine, misty rain, while heavier rains fall from October to March. Winters (July through October) tend to be dry, with cold air coming up to the plateau from the ocean and often producing fog.

Mean temperature varies from a low of 17.8 C (64F) in July to 21.8 C (71F) in March. Mean rainfall ranges from 17.9mm (.7 inches) in July to 127.8mm (5 inches) in December. (1961-1990 trends from Hong Kong Observatories).

The vegetation ranges from very dry and coarse (1000 meters and above) to an array of grasses, ferns and palms in slightly lower elevations on the plateau. This is the coffee-growing elevation. (MEDEIROS, Ruy H. A. - Notas Críticas ao livro "O Município da Vitória"de Tranquilino Torres, p.87)

Foundation

Vitória da Conquista was founded in 1783, after several battles against the native Imboré and Mongoió tribes by João Gonçalves da Costa, born in Chaves, Trás-os-Montes, Portugal.

Costa had been sent to Brazil by the king of Portugal, Joseph I, to fight against the natives, conquer their land, and then convert them to Christianity. He founded The Arraial da Conquista ("Conquest Town") on the site of the last battle and began the building of a church in honour of the Holy Mother of Victory.

At the same time, João Gonçalves da Costa ordered the construction of two of the main roads in the state of Bahia, one from Vitória da Conquista to Ilhéus and another from Vitória da Conquista to River Jequitinhonha in Minas Gerais. Today this second road has become part of a much longer federal highway known as the *Rio-Bahia*.

Business and commerce

The major economic activities are commerce, medical services, and coffee growing. The city is becoming a university center, mainly due to the establishment and growth of State University of Southeast of Bahia.

The business atmosphere is energetic and in full blown expansion mode. From larger businesses such as Grupo Marinho de Andrade (Teiú e Revani), Coca-Cola, Dilly Calçados (shoes), Umbro, BahiaFarma, Café Maratá, to the smallest cottage industries, the area continues to attract strong interest.

The entrepreneurial Ymborés Industrial Center (Centro Industrial dos Ymborés) lies on the outskirts of the city with industries such as ceramics, marble, shoes, toilet valves, cleaning, bedding, and many others. Micro industries produce safes, candles, clothing, packaging, and hundreds of other products for local consumption and export. As a business center, Vitoria da Conquista serves the entire southwest region of the state of Bahia and the northern part of the state of Minas Gerais.

Ilhéus

The Municipality of São Jorge dos Ilhéos
— Municipality —
Beach in Ilhéus (June 2006)
Nickname(s): *Princesinha do Sul* (Little Princess of the South)
Location of Ilhéus
Coordinates: 14°47′20″S 39°02′56″W

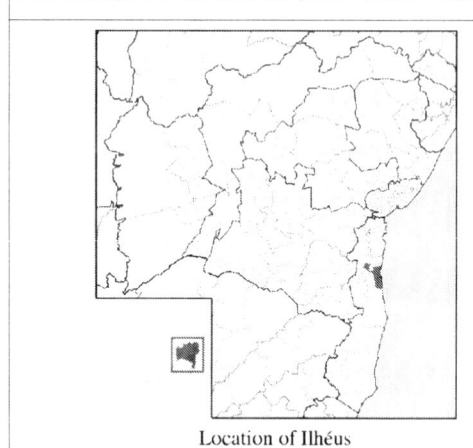

Region	Nordeste
State	Bahia
Founded	28 June 1881
Government	
- Mayor	Newton Lima

Area	
- Total	1840.991 km² (710.8 sq mi)
Elevation	52 m (171 ft)
Population (2006)	
- Total	220943
- Density	120/km² (310.8/sq mi)

Ilhéus is a major city located in the southern coastal region of Bahia, Brazil, 430 km south of Salvador, the state's capital. The city was originally founded in 1534 as Vila de São Jorge dos Ilhéus and is known as one of the most important tourism centers of the northeast of Brazil.

The city's economy is based mainly on tourism, as a result of its beautiful beaches and a rich cultural heritage that includes early Portuguese buildings, history and culinary distinctions, which bring to the city many Brazilian and foreign tourists. Ilheus has approximately 222,000 inhabitants, with an area of 1850 km sq, and its downtown is located 1 km away from the Atlantic Ocean. Once one of the biggest exporters of cocoa beans, the city depends almost entirely on tourism. Ilhéus has a very good infrastructure for tourism, including excellent hotels and many travel agencies.

Ilhéus is easily reachable by air with multiple flights daily from both Salvador and São Paulo on TAM Brazilian Airlines and Gol Linhas Aéreas.

Ilhéus is also the hometown of Jorge Amado, the best known and most popular writer in Brazil. He wrote over 25 novels, which were translated into 48 languages and stayed on bestseller lists in 52 countries. His novels like *Gabriela, Clove and Cinnamon* and *Dona Flor and Her Two Husbands* portray life and customs in the Northeastern region of Brazil. The plots of these and his other major works largely treat the lives of poor urban and rural black and mulatto communities of Bahia, as well as the land wars that raged in Ilhéus, where cocoa barons killed each other for power and cocoa plantations.

Attractions

Beaches

Do Norte (Northern Beach)

Mixing a strip of coconut trees with rich vegetation of native Atlantic Forest, running parallel to the beach for many kilometers there is the Almada River. There visitors will find standardized stalls and a very long bicycle lane. It is a good place for swimming, walking, surfing, and fishing.

São Miguel (da Barra) (Saint Michael's Beach – Beach of the Sandbank)

It is a beautiful beach, with a vast area of coconut trees, clear sands, and calm waters. The infrastructure on the beach includes stalls and lodges located in the local fishermen's village.

Da Avenida (Beach of the Avenue)

Centrally located, its main attractions are on the seashore, where many facilities have been built, such as multiple-activity sports courts, a bike lane, a band shell, the "Folias da Gabriela" circus, and the Luís Eduardo Magalhães Conventions Center.

Do Cristo (Christ's Beach)

As its very name indicates, there is a statue of the Redeeming Christ on this very popular beach for tourists. Its waters are recommended for various water sports, such as kayaking, jet-skiing, and hobby-cat sailing.

Da Concha (Shell's Beach)

A small-sized beach, with a total width of only 100 meters (about 330 feet). From there, tourists have a good view of the Baía do Pontal (End Beach) and of the Avenida Beach (Beach of the Avenue). Located at the base of Pernambuco Hill, it still has areas of native vegetation mixed with many coconut trees. Its waters are calm, ideal for swimming.

Do Sul (Southern Beach)

Having as its main characteristic a thick field of coconut trees and traces of the native Atlantic Forest, this urban beach is one of the busies beaches in the city. Along its whole length tourists will find a great number of food stalls, most of which specialize in the typical dishes of the state of Bahia. In the sea, stretches of reefs and natural swimming pools with sandy bottoms are greatly sought by divers and surfers.

Dos Milionários (Millionaires' Beach)

Its name is a direct consequence of the fact that it was formerly the beach of choice of the rich cocoa "colonels" (local farm owners, caudillos). Today, it is the most desired beach on the south coast, by swimmers and tourists alike, who love its very long strip of sand bordered by a row of coconut trees. Its infrastructure includes a camping site, several standardized stalls, showers, and rest rooms.

Cururupe

A rich beach in number of growths of mangroves, it also has rental huts and kayaks. It also has great historical importance, because it was the stage of a fierce battle in 1559, which destroyed almost completely the village of the Brazilian Indians.

Back Door

The first beach of the Olivença district, the Back Door beach is characterized by its enormous waves. Because of this, the beach has become the beach of choice for the most important surfing championships held in the state of Bahia.

Batuba

Its landscape is a mix of vast areas of coconut trees and many reefs. It is a very busy beach, much appreciated by surfers. There are several adjacent restaurants specializing in seafood. There is also a good camping site, with all the usual facilities.

Cai N'água (Milagres) (Fall in the Water – Miracles Beach)

With well equipped stalls, many swimming areas of clear still water, this beach is perfect for the enjoyment of families. It is located within the zone of the settlement with the same name, and contains many summer vacation houses as well.

Canabrava

One of the favorite beaches for vacationers, on the beach there are countless rental houses and cottages. Its landscape is a mix of coconut tree fields, coral reefs, and large resorts.

Acuípe

This beach has a very special landscape, with a mix of sandbank vegetation and a beautiful spread of coconut trees. In Acuípe, tourists will find several hotels and lodges offering visitors an excellent infrastructure. The beach is good for walking, sea bathing, and reel fishing.

In Town

Museu Casa de Cultura Jorge Amado (Jorge Amado House of Culture Museum)

The estate was bought by Colonel João Amado, father of Jorge Amado, the most famous writer of the state of Bahia. There, the Colonel built his large beautiful house, with spacious lounges decorated in jacaranda wood and Carrara marble. Its construction started at the beginning of the 1920s, and was finished in 1926. The famous writer spent part of his life here. The house has also been used as the headquarters of the Clube dos Bancários (Club of the Bank Employees), and of the Faculdade de Direito de Ilhéus (Ilhéus College of Law). Today, it houses the Fundação Cultural de Ilhéus (Ilhéus Cultural Foundation) and the Casa de Jorge Amado (Jorge Amado's House). The building is a cultural centre that pays homage to the writer and whose main objective is the advancement of local culture.

Jorge Amado de Faria (August 10, 1912 – August 6, 2001) was a Brazilian writer of the Modernist school. He was the best-known of modern Brazilian writers, his work having been translated into some 30 languages and popularized in film, notably Dona Flor and her Two Husbands (Dona Flor e Seus Dois Maridos) in 1978. His work dealt largely with the poor urban black and mulatto communities of Bahia.

São Jorge de Ilhéus Church (Saint George of Ilhéus Church)

This church dates back to the end of the seventeenth century, according to the Instituto do Patrimônio Artístico e Cultural do Estado da Bahia – IPAC/BA (Institute of the Artistic and Cultural Patrimony of the State of Bahia). The church is the seat of the Roman Catholic Diocese of Ilhéus.

Sacred Art Museum

It is located next to the São Jorge de Ilhéus Church. Its collection includes a secular statue of Saint George, sacred documents, valuable items and objects from the sixteenth, seventeenth, and eighteenth centuries, and a panel portraying the history of Ilhéus. The museum is supported by the Metropolitan Curia.

Bar Vesúvio (Vesuvius Bar)

The Bar Vesúvio (Vesuvius Bar) has been one of the most visited places in the town ever since its creation, at the end of the 1920s, when it was frequented by cocoa farmers who would meet their friends and recount their stories and love conquests. Many visitors and tourists who drop by know it from the Jorge Amado novel Gabriela, Cravo e Canela (Gabriela, Clove and Cinnamon), and who come to savor the famous "Nacib's kibbeh" – one of dishes most referred to in the novel, in which Mr. Nacib is the owner of the Vesuvius bar, the place where young Gabriela works.

Ecoparque de Una (Una's Ecopark)

At 19 km (11.81 mi.) from the Una Biological Reservation, in a journey that passes by the beautiful beaches of the Southern coast of Ihéus, the Una Ecopark begins in the middle of a rubber plantation where visitors can see the manual extraction of the sap of the rubber tree. Trails in the park take visitors to a suspended footbridge, of some 20 meters (65.62 feet) of height, in the crown of the trees, with a privileged view of the Atlantic Forest. During the ride, often are tourists dazzled with the "visit" of the nice Golden Lion Tamarins. The final prize is a refreshing bath in the waters of the Maruim River. This ride requires its prior scheduling with the Instituto Brasileiro do Meio Ambiente e dos Recursos Naturais Renováveis – IBAMA (Brazilian Institute of the Environment and the Renewable Natural Resources).

Mata da Esperança Botanical Garden (Hope Woods Botanical Garden)

With an immense variety of species of the Atlantic Forest, the Mata da Esperança Park – today the Botanical Garden – represents a place of resistance and preservation of the native fauna and flora of the area. Either form bicycle or on foot, visitors can cover its trails, having a unique possibility of enjoying the wonders kept there, such as the Golden-headed Lion Tamarin.

Engenho da Esperança (Esperança Sugar Mill)

Around the sixteenth century, in the area where today is the Botanical Garden there was the Engenho da Esperança (Esperança Sugar Mill). It is worth paying the place a visit to see its ruins and learn about the histories of the place's past. The company of a guide to show the ways and guide the hikes is fundamental. In the town's center, tourists may rent bicycles. With them, the whole ride, which lasts some three hours on foot, is reduced to only one hour.

Centro de Recuperação do Bicho-Preguiça (Sloth Recovery Center)

The center is located within the area of Atlantic Forest, in the Centro Educativo da Natureza (Educational Center of the Nature). That center, which serves to both recover and re-introduce species of sloth into its natural habitat, won the 1998 Prêmio Natureza (1998 Nature Prize). The animals of the

Centro de Recuperação (Recovery Center) dazzle visitors because of how much they resemble plush animals, and for their friendliness in the contact with humans. During the rides, which last four hours on the average, it is possible to see other species of animals and plants, natural to the Atlantic Forest. To visit the Center, tourists have to schedule the visit in advance, calling the center at +55 73 3214-3014/3016/3013.

Transport

- Road: BR-101 connects it to Itabuna and beyond.
- Air: Ilhéus Jorge Amado Airport with daily flights of TAM, GOL and Webjet

with destinations Belo Horizonte-Confins (CNF), Brasília (BSB), Porto Seguro (BPS), Rio de Janeiro-Galeão (GIG), Salvador (SSA), São Paulo-Guarulhos (GRU).

- Sea: Port of Ilhéus.

External links

- Ilhéus Virtual [1] (in Portuguese)
- A Região, notícias de Ilhéus [2] (in Portuguese)
- Verao.com - Guia de Ilhéus e região [3] (in Portuguese)
- Brasilheus [4] (site in English and Portuguese)
- Brasil Destinos [5] (in Portuguese)

Itabuna

Itabuna

State	Bahia
Area	443.2 km²
Population Population density	209,221 (2006) 462,5 inhab/km²
Altitude	54 meters above the sea level
Latitude	14°47'09"S
Longitude	39°16'48" W
Distance from Salvador	416 km
URL:	http://www.itabuna.ba.gov.br
City mayor	José Nilton Azevedo Leal
Map	

Itabuna is a city in Bahia, Brazil. Located around 14°47'09"S 39°16'48"W, it's the 5th city in Bahia, after Salvador, Feira de Santana, Vitória da Conquista, and Ilhéus, in size of population, with an estimative of 209,211 inhabitants in 2006. The city covers a total area of 443.2 km².

Itabuna became a city separated from Ilhéus in 1910. In 1978, the city became the seat of the Roman Catholic Diocese of Itabuna.

Economy

Itabuna is a regional center of commerce, industry and services, along with its neighbour Ilhéus. Its economic importance grew during the *golden era* of cocoa cultivation. Thanks to its fertile soil, the city became the second biggest producer of cocoa in Brazil, exporting to the United States and Europe. After the devastation of crops caused by the fungus *Crinipellis perniciosa* (which causes a disease known as witch's broom), which led to a profound crisis in its economy, the city began to search a diversification of its economical activities.

Nowadays, Itabuna one of the most important tradepoints located along BR-101 Highway in Bahia.

Jequié

Jequié is a city in the state of Bahia, Brazil. It is located at around 13°51′3″S 40°4′52″W. It is nicknamed "A cidade do sol", or "The city of the Sun" because of its high temperatures.

Lauro de Freitas

Lauro de Freitas is a municipality of 59 km² in the north-east of the state of Bahia, Brasil located at 12° 53' 38" South 38° 19' 37" West. In Lauro de Freitas is located Vilas do Atlântico, a wealthy neighborhood. As of 2005, there are 141.280 inhabitants.

Geographical coordinates: 12°53'38"S 38°19'37"W

Cachoeira

Coat of arms	
Statistics	
State:	Bahia
Meso-region:	Metropolitana de Salvador
Micro-Region:	Santo Antônio de Jesus
Founded:	January 1, 1939
Location:	12°37'4"S 38°57'21"W
Area:	398.472 km²
Population:	31,966(2006)
Population density:	80.22/km²
Postal code:	44300-xxx
Distance from the state capital:	110 km north
Name of inhabitants:	*cachoeirense*
Other	
Climate:	tropical

Cachoeira (Portuguese, meaning the waterfall), is an inland town of Bahia, Brazil, on the Paraguaçu River. The town exports sugar, cotton and tobacco and is a thriving commercial and industrial centre.

First settled by the Indians, it was later settled by the Portuguese families of Dias Adorno and Rodrigues Martins. It became known as Nossa Senhora do Rosário in 1674. It was a strategic area and was linked with the mining city of Salvador, the former colonial capital. It became a parish on December 27, 1693. It also became Vila de Nossa Senhora do Rosário do Porto da Cachoeira do Paraguaçu in 1698.

Sugar cane farming, gold mining on rio das Contas, increased traffic on royal streets, and navigation on the Rio Paraguaçu combined to boost the regional economy in the beginning of the 18th century. In the beginning of 1800, the Cachoeirense society became very important politically. It actively participated in the war of the Independence of Bahia.

The town became a city under the imperial decree of March 13, 1873 (Provincial Law 43).

Cachoeira is considered a national monument of the Instituto do Patrimônio Histórico Artístico e Nacional (IPHAN)

It is currently undergoing a bit of a tourist revival, and is a centre of candomblé.

Population history

Year	Population	Change	Density
1890	12,607	-	-
2004	31,071	-	77.98/km²
2006	31,966	-	80.22/km²

References

This article incorporates a translation from the Portuguese Wikipedia

External links

- (Portuguese) http://www.citybrazil.com.br/ba/cachoeira/
- (Portuguese) iCachoeira.com [1]
- (Portuguese) Hotels in Bahia [2]
- (Portuguese) Brazilian Touristic Portal [3]

Juazeiro

Juazeiro is a city and municipality in eastern Brazil in the state of Bahia (9°25′S 40°30′W). It had a population of 198,065, according to the 2004 census, and an area of 6,415.4 km². The population density was 31.34 hab/km² (2000). The elevation is 373 meters. It became a city in 1833. [1]

Although it lies on the São Francisco River and the Curaçá River, the climate of the city is semi-arid and it gets an annual precipitation of only 399 mm. For more detailed information on the climate see Petrolina

There are highway connections with several capitals of the Northeast and railroad connections to the coast are made by the Ferrovia Centro-Atlântic. The railroad connection ends at the fluvial port of Juazeiro.

The name comes from the juazeiro tree (Ziziphus joazeiro) which grows in the region.

Juazeiro is in reality part of a twin city called Petrolina-Juazeiro making an urban conglomerate of close to 500,000 inhabitants. The two cities are connected by a modern bridge crossing the São Francisco River.

It was founded in 1833 and became a city on July 15, 1878. The annual average temperature is 24.2 °C. Its city districts are Abóbora, Carnaíba, Itamotinga, Junco, Juremal, Massaroca, and Pinhões.

Like its sister city Petrolina, Juazeiro has experienced great growth in the last decade due to the irrigation of the semi-arid soils with water from the São Francisco River. Fruit cultivation is important to such extent that Juazeiro entitles itself "Capital of Irrigated Fruit", which its exported between the Petrolina Airport to USA and/or Europe. For more detailed information on the development of this fertile valley see the article on Petrolina.

Juazeiro is the birthplace of Brazil and Barcelona footballer Dani Alves. Main agricultural products in planted area (2003):

- bananas: 18 km²
- coconut: 2.72 km²
- guava: 2.5 km²
- lemon: 2 km²
- papaya: 0.45 km²
- mango: 60 km²
- passion fruit: 0.9 km²
- grapes: 21 km²
- sugarcane: 152.53 km²
- onions: 3.4 km²
- beans: 4.04 km²
- manioc: 4.2 km²

- watermelon: 4.5 km²
- melon: 1.95 km²
- tomato: 0.32 km²

Data is from IBGE [2]

This city should not be confused with Juazeiro do Piauí or Juazeiro do Norte, also cities in Brazil.

External links

- Prefeitura Municipal de Juazeiro [3]

Transportation

Deputado Luís Eduardo Magalhães International Airport

Salvador-Deputado Luís Eduardo Magalhães International Airport (2 de Julho)
Aeroporto Internacional de Salvador-Deputado Luís Eduardo Magalhães (2 de Julho)

IATA: SSA – ICAO: SBSV

Summary

Airport type	Public/Military
Operator	Infraero
Serves	Salvador da Bahia
Hub for	{{{hub}}}
Elevation AMSL	20 m / 64 ft
Coordinates	12°54′39″S 38°19′51″W
Website	Infraero SSA [1]

Runways

Direction	Length (m)	Length (ft)	Surface
10/28	3,005	9,859	Asphalt
17/35	1,519	4,985	Asphalt

Statistics (2009)

Passengers	7,052,720
Aircraft Operations	102,211
Metric tonnes of cargo	36,981

Statistics: Infraero
Sources: Airport Website

Salvador-Deputado Luís Eduardo Magalhães International Airport (IATA: **SSA**, ICAO: **SBSV**), more commonly known as it was formerly named: **Dois de Julho International Airport**. It is located in Salvador, Bahia, Brazil. It is administered by Infraero, and lies 20 km (12 mi) north of downtown Salvador. The airport is located in an area of more than 6 million square meters between sand dunes and native vegetation. The road route to the airport has already become one of the city's main scenic attractions. In 2008, the airport handled 6,042,307 passengers and 95,804 aircraft movements, placing it 5th busiest airport in Brazil in terms of passengers.

The airport's use has been growing at an average of 14% a year and now is responsible for more than 30% of passenger movement in Brazil's Northeast. Nearly 35 thousand people circulate daily through the passenger terminal. The airport generates more than 16 thousand direct and indirect jobs, to serve a daily average of over 10 thousand passengers, 250 takeoffs and landings of 100 domestic and 16 international flights.

Many of these flights are domestic flights from within Brazil where Salvador serves as a major transfer point for flights to and from smaller cities throughout the Northeastern Brazil. Salvador International Airport has international service to North America, South America, Europe, and Africa.

History

The airport was founded in 1925, and was completely rebuilt in 1941 by Panair do Brasil ("necessities of war", declared the American and the Brazilian governments). Its old name was Santo Amaro do Ipitanga. In 1955, the airport changed its name to *Dois de Julho*, and, in 1998, to the present name, although Salvador's inhabitants mostly continue to refer to the airport by the older name *Dois de Julho*, which commemorates Bahia Independence Day.

On 31 August 2009 Infraero unveiled an ambitious BRL5.3 billion (USD2.8 billion; EUR2.0 billion) investment plan to renovate and upgrade airports of ten cities focusing on the preparations for the 2014 FIFA World Cup which will be held in Brazil. At the occasion it was announced that even though they are venue cities, the plan excluded Salvador and Natal airports because renovations had been recently completed and Infraero considered the airports fit to handle the forthcoming increases in traffic.

General information

- Main terminal: 69,400 m²
- Number of jetways: 11
- Capacity: 6,000,000 passengers
- Direct jobs: 4,000

Airlines and destinations

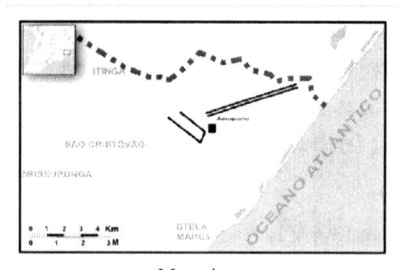

Map view.

Airlines	Destinations
Abaeté Linhas Aéreas	Bom Jesus da Lapa, Guanambi
Aerolíneas Argentinas	Buenos Aires-Aeroparque [ends 19 October; resumes 6 December], Buenos Aires-Ezeiza [begins 20 October; ends 5 December]
Air Italy	Milan-Malpensa
American Airlines	Miami
Avianca Brazil	Brasília, Petrolina, Recife, São Paulo-Guarulhos
Azul Brazilian Airlines	Belo Horizonte-Confins, Campinas-Viracopos, Porto Alegre, Rio de Janeiro-Santos Dumont, Vitória
Condor	Frankfurt
Iberworld	Madrid
Gol Airlines	Aracaju, Belém-Val de Cães, Belo Horizonte-Confins, Brasília, Campinas-Viracopos, Cuiabá, Fortaleza, Ilhéus, João Pessoa, Maceió, Manaus, Natal, Porto Alegre, Porto Seguro, Recife, Rio de Janeiro-Galeão, Rio de Janeiro-Santos Dumont, São Luís, São Paulo-Congonhas, São Paulo-Guarulhos
Passaredo	Brasília, Barreiras, Ribeirão Preto, São Paulo-Guarulhos, Vitória da Conquista
TAM Airlines	Belém-Val de Cães, Belo Horizonte-Confins, Brasília, Buenos Aires-Ezeiza, Campinas-Viracopos, Curitiba-Afonso Pena, Fortaleza, Foz do Iguaçu, Ilhéus, João Pessoa, Manaus, Natal, Porto Alegre, Porto Seguro, Recife, Rio de Janeiro-Galeão, Rio de Janeiro-Santos Dumont, Santarém, São Luís, São Paulo-Congonhas, São Paulo-Guarulhos
TAM Airlines operated by Pantanal Linhas Aéreas	Rio de Janeiro-Galeão, São Paulo-Congonhas
TAP Portugal	Lisbon

TRIP Linhas Aéreas	Aracaju, Belo Horizonte-Confins, Fernando de Noronha, Ilhéus, Lençóis, Natal, Petrolina, Recife, Vitória, Vitória da Conquista
Webjet	Belo Horizonte-Confins, Brasília, Curitiba-Afonso Pena, Fortaleza, Porto Alegre, Recife, Rio de Janeiro-Galeão
XL Airways France [a]	Paris-Charles de Gaulle, Sal

a. Airline operating regular charter flights.

Accidents and incidents

Accidents with fatalities

- 21 September 1944: Panair do Brasil, a Lockheed Model 18 Lodestar registration PP-PBH crashed shortly after take-off from Salvador. All 17 occupants died.
- 30 May 1950: Aerovias Brasil, a Douglas C-47-DL registration PP-AVZ, en route from Vitória da Conquista to Salvador disintegrated on air, while flying over Itacaré, near Ilhéus. It was flying under extremely bad conditions and entered a cumulus nimbus. Passengers and cargo were moved aboard and as a consequence control was lost. Both wings separated from the aircraft as it descended at great speed. Of the 15 passengers and crew aboard, 2 survived.

Incidents

- 15 May 1973: VASP, a Vickers Viscount registration PP-SRD was damaged beyond economic repair when it departed the runway on landing and the undercarriage collapsed.

See also

- List of the busiest airports in Brazil

References

This article incorporates public domain material from websites or documents [2] *of the Air Force Historical Research Agency.*

External links

- Airport information for SBSV [1] at World Aero Data. Data current as of October 2006. Source: DAFIF.
- Airport information for SBSV [2] at Great Circle Mapper. Source: DAFIF (effective Oct. 2006).
- Current weather for SBSV [3] at NOAA/NWS
- Accident history for SSA [4] at Aviation Safety Network

Salvador Metro

Salvador Metro	
Info	
Locale	Salvador, Bahia
Transit type	Rapid transit
Number of lines	2
Number of stations	8
Operation	
Began operation	July, 2011
Operator(s)	Companhia de Transportes de Salvador
Technical	
System length	12 km (7.4 mi)

The **Salvador Metro** (Portuguese: *Metrô de Salvador*, commonly called *Metrô*) is a metro system of the city of Salvador, Brazil. The Line 1 runs from the Lapa to Cajazeiras, with metro stations in Pólvora, Brotas, Bonocô, Acesso Norte, Retiro, Juá, Pirajá, Mata Escura and Pau de Lima. Already the Line 2 runs from Calçada Futura to Mussurunga, with metro stations in Água de Meninos, Dois Leões, Acesso Norte, Bus Station in Iguatemi, Imbuí and Administrative Center of Bahia.

The project is a Build, Operate, and Transfer (BOT) scheme for the operation of the urban rapid rail transportation system in the municipality of Salvador da Bahia, and includes the supply and installation of rolling stock and signaling equipment, and commercial operation of the system for the 25-year concession. Each train, consisting of four cars, has the capacity to carry 1,250 passengers.

Currently, the urban transportation system in Salvador is underdeveloped and largely road-based, causing significant congestion and delays. This level of road-based transport has significant impacts on the local economy and environment. For this reason the municipality and the state, together with the World Bank, have been involved since 1992 in the design and implementation of a transportation strategy. The international standard gauge is 3kV overhead power supply. And Built by a consortium of

Siemens and Camargo Corrêa and Andrade Gutierrez of Brazil.

This project is an integral part of the strategy. The project aims to improve the quality of public urban transportation in the area by connecting currently-excluded low-income neighborhoods, and by furthering the development of a fully integrated urban transportation system.

Salvador Metro system is one of the actions of urban mobility that will be deployed until the 2014 FIFA World Cup. Besides the subway, the city government is developing a project for integrated mass transport will be composed of so-called Bus Rapid Transit in Brazil (BRT), the subway and bus routes exclusive. The system will make the integration between the stations of the Rótula do Abacaxi and the beach city of Lauro de Freitas in the metropolitan area, passing through the Salvador International Airport.

The Line 1 connects to the Transfer of Lapa, the largest of Salvador, to Rótula do Abacaxi, passing by Fonte Nova Stadium, the official stadium of FIFA World Cup, the stadium has a metro station of Line 1. Also in this Line of the Metro exist the junction between the main avenues of Salvador with the busiest highway in the State of Bahia, BR-324, in the area of Rótula do Abacaxi, which connects the city to Feira de Santana. Also located on the local, the Bus station of Salvador, the largest of Bahia, which is located across from the Iguatemi Mall, and the most important Central Business District of Salvador, in the area of Iguatemi.

Lines

Line	Terminals	Extension	Inauguration	Distance (km)	Stations	Time (min)	Situation
1	Lapa ↔ Pirajá	Pirajá ↔ Cajazeiras**	2011	20.1	8*(11)**	12 min	In construction.
2	Calçada ↔ Mussurunga	---	---	23.9	8	---	In project.
Suburban Train	Calçada ↔ Paripe	---	2005	13.5	9	25 min	Daily, 05:00 AM - 11:00 PM.

(*) Stations in construction • (**) In project

See also

- List of rapid transit systems

Port of Salvador

The Port of Salvador	
Map view of The Port of Salvador	
Location	
Country	Brazil
Location	Salvador, Bahia
Coordinates	12°57'31"S 38°30'27"W
Details	
Opened	1502
Operated by	Companhia das Docas do Estado da Bahia (CODEBA)
Type of harbor	Harbor
Size	Medium
President	Jose Muniz Rebouças
Statistics	
Vessel arrivals	1,027
Website	The Port of Salvador [1]

The **Port of Salvador** is a seaport located in All Saints Bay in Salvador, Bahia, Brazil. It is connected to Downtown Salvador by Historic Center. The port is located in Lower City region of Salvador. Lying at the tip of a peninsula separating Todos os Santos Bay from the Atlantic Ocean.

CODEBA was established to manage and distribute cargoes throughout the State of Bahia. To assure effective operations, CODEBA seeks to provide modern infrastructure and technological support to the Port of Salvador.

In 2007 over 3 million tons of cargo moved through the Port of Salvador, including 2.6 million tons of ocean-going cargo and 530 thousand tons of internal cargo. The same year, the Port of Salvador handled 1.6 tons of container exports in 73 thousand TEUs and 753 thousand tons in container imports in 71 thousand TEUs. Further, the Port of Salvador greeted 88 cruise vessels carrying 1421 passengers.

The modern Port of Salvador is connected to inland Brazil by rail, road, and air. Its sheltered harbor is protected from tidal fluctuations. Two canals bring ocean-going vessels into the port. The anchoring area is 700 meters wide with depths from 9 to 12 meters. Major imports through the Port of Salvador are wheat and grains, foods, chemical products, equipment, vehicles, and malt. Major exports include petrochemical and iron products, granite, fruits and sisal, cellulose, copper, and vehicles.

History

Europeans first saw what was to become the Port of Salvador in 1502. In 1549, Portuguese settlers led by Brazil's first Governor-General, Tome de Sousa, established the new town. It became the seat of Brazil's first Catholic bishopric in 1552, and by 1583, over 1600 people lived there. At the time of the American Revolution in the late 18th century, the Port of Salvador was bigger than any American city. The busy port was a target for pirates and privateers. Dutch soldiers captured it in 1624, but the Portuguese retook the Port of Salvador the next year, holding it until Brazilian independence in 1823. In 1763, the seat of the colonial government was moved to Rio de Janeiro, and the Port of Salvador entered an era of decline that lasted until the 20th Century.

The 1940s brought economic and population growth to the Port of Salvador. By 1948, almost 350 thousand people lived there. When an industrial center and petrochemical complex were built nearby in the early 1970s, the need for a modern port became clear. The first terminal at the Port of Salvador was opened in 1975. The 1990s brought city clean-up and restoration efforts to the Port of Salvador. The old downtown area, called Pelourinho, was restored to become the city's cultural center. Although the city center is now a UNESCO World Heritage Site, it remains relatively empty. Local merchants often import events and activity to animate the area.

Article Sources and Contributors

Bahia *Source*: http://en.wikipedia.org/?oldid=386834848 *Contributors*: 1 anonymous edits

Samba *Source*: http://en.wikipedia.org/?oldid=389849779 *Contributors*:

Capoeira *Source*: http://en.wikipedia.org/?oldid=390414374 *Contributors*: 1 anonymous edits

Salvador, Bahia *Source*: http://en.wikipedia.org/?oldid=390153980 *Contributors*: Hentzer

Barra (neighborhood) *Source*: http://en.wikipedia.org/?oldid=382952823 *Contributors*: Hentzer

Brotas (neighbourhood) *Source*: http://en.wikipedia.org/?oldid=383790653 *Contributors*: WhisperToMe

Cajazeiras (neighbourhood) *Source*: http://en.wikipedia.org/?oldid=383943653 *Contributors*:

Caminho das Árvores (neighbourhood) *Source*: http://en.wikipedia.org/?oldid=304495717 *Contributors*: Berger1

Campo Grande (neighbourhood) *Source*: http://en.wikipedia.org/?oldid=338024354 *Contributors*: 1 anonymous edits

Graça (neighborhood) *Source*: http://en.wikipedia.org/?oldid=343737848 *Contributors*:

Historic Centre (Salvador, Bahia) *Source*: http://en.wikipedia.org/?oldid=362785206 *Contributors*: Jmhullot

Itaigara (neighbourhood) *Source*: http://en.wikipedia.org/?oldid=366213805 *Contributors*: 1 anonymous edits

Itapoã (neighbourhood) *Source*: http://en.wikipedia.org/?oldid=325405532 *Contributors*: JaGa

Liberdade (neighbourhood) *Source*: http://en.wikipedia.org/?oldid=355685405 *Contributors*: 1 anonymous edits

Ondina (neighbourhood) *Source*: http://en.wikipedia.org/?oldid=357223381 *Contributors*: R'n'B

Pituba (neighbourhood) *Source*: http://en.wikipedia.org/?oldid=356388721 *Contributors*: R'n'B

Rio Vermelho (neighbourhood) *Source*: http://en.wikipedia.org/?oldid=384039983 *Contributors*: AKeen

Vitória (neighbourhood) *Source*: http://en.wikipedia.org/?oldid=382921699 *Contributors*: Hmains

Periperi *Source*: http://en.wikipedia.org/?oldid=298189206 *Contributors*: Rich Farmbrough

Museu Rodin Bahia *Source*: http://en.wikipedia.org/?oldid=273635964 *Contributors*:

Cathedral of Salvador *Source*: http://en.wikipedia.org/?oldid=366140821 *Contributors*: Look2See1

São Francisco Church and Convent *Source*: http://en.wikipedia.org/?oldid=382863096 *Contributors*:

Church of Nosso Senhor do Bonfim, Salvador *Source*: http://en.wikipedia.org/?oldid=379300918 *Contributors*:

September Seven Avenue *Source*: http://en.wikipedia.org/?oldid=320526505 *Contributors*:

Oceanic Avenue *Source*: http://en.wikipedia.org/?oldid=335548365 *Contributors*: TheTito

Bahian Carnival *Source*: http://en.wikipedia.org/?oldid=385353176 *Contributors*: Luan

Grande Sertão Veredas National Park *Source*: http://en.wikipedia.org/?oldid=332031901 *Contributors*:

Abrolhos Marine National Park *Source*: http://en.wikipedia.org/?oldid=390217602 *Contributors*: პაატა შ

Chapada Diamantina National Park *Source*: http://en.wikipedia.org/?oldid=388596797 *Contributors*: Hmains

Morro de São Paulo *Source*: http://en.wikipedia.org/?oldid=383293953 *Contributors*:

Itaparica Island *Source*: http://en.wikipedia.org/?oldid=334902218 *Contributors*: DerBorg

Sincura *Source*: http://en.wikipedia.org/?oldid=366794115 *Contributors*: 1 anonymous edits

Porto da Barra Beach *Source*: http://en.wikipedia.org/?oldid=387079434 *Contributors*: Guslacerda

Baía de Todos os Santos *Source*: http://en.wikipedia.org/?oldid=382993342 *Contributors*:

Esporte Clube Bahia *Source*: http://en.wikipedia.org/?oldid=388132608 *Contributors*: LobãoV

Galícia Esporte Clube *Source*: http://en.wikipedia.org/?oldid=383987878 *Contributors*: Александр Мотин

Associação Desportiva Leônico *Source*: http://en.wikipedia.org/?oldid=378694171 *Contributors*:

Esporte Clube Vitória *Source*: http://en.wikipedia.org/?oldid=390579853 *Contributors*: 1 anonymous edits

Esporte Clube Ypiranga *Source*: http://en.wikipedia.org/?oldid=387138714 *Contributors*: 1 anonymous edits

Article Sources and Contributors

ATP Itaparica *Source*: http://en.wikipedia.org/?oldid=378146292 *Contributors*: Coyets

Estádio Parque Santiago *Source*: http://en.wikipedia.org/?oldid=277964260 *Contributors*:

Estádio de Pituaçu *Source*: http://en.wikipedia.org/?oldid=376492331 *Contributors*:

Estádio Fonte Nova *Source*: http://en.wikipedia.org/?oldid=388509568 *Contributors*: Miller17CU94

Barradão *Source*: http://en.wikipedia.org/?oldid=385185085 *Contributors*:

Porto Seguro *Source*: http://en.wikipedia.org/?oldid=388177054 *Contributors*: Hmains

Feira de Santana *Source*: http://en.wikipedia.org/?oldid=375699638 *Contributors*:

Vitória da Conquista *Source*: http://en.wikipedia.org/?oldid=388761017 *Contributors*:

Ilhéus *Source*: http://en.wikipedia.org/?oldid=387966930 *Contributors*: R'n'B

Itabuna *Source*: http://en.wikipedia.org/?oldid=385189970 *Contributors*: Timdress

Jequié *Source*: http://en.wikipedia.org/?oldid=381356448 *Contributors*:

Lauro de Freitas *Source*: http://en.wikipedia.org/?oldid=390092567 *Contributors*: 1 anonymous edits

Cachoeira *Source*: http://en.wikipedia.org/?oldid=382116125 *Contributors*:

Juazeiro *Source*: http://en.wikipedia.org/?oldid=381369310 *Contributors*:

Deputado Luís Eduardo Magalhães International Airport *Source*: http://en.wikipedia.org/?oldid=390475137 *Contributors*: Brunoptsem

Salvador Metro *Source*: http://en.wikipedia.org/?oldid=385252467 *Contributors*: Hentzer

Port of Salvador *Source*: http://en.wikipedia.org/?oldid=385489475 *Contributors*: Hmains

Image Sources, Licenses and Contributors

File:Brasão da Bahia.png *Source*: http://bibliocm.bibliolabs.com/mwAnon/index.php?title=File:Brasão_da_Bahia.png *License*: unknown *Contributors*: -

File:Brazil State Bahia.svg *Source*: http://bibliocm.bibliolabs.com/mwAnon/index.php?title=File:Brazil_State_Bahia.svg *License*: unknown *Contributors*: -

Image:Salvador-CCBY-5.jpg *Source*: http://bibliocm.bibliolabs.com/mwAnon/index.php?title=File:Salvador-CCBY-5.jpg *License*: unknown *Contributors*: -

Image:BonfimSalvador-CCBY.jpg *Source*: http://bibliocm.bibliolabs.com/mwAnon/index.php?title=File:BonfimSalvador-CCBY.jpg *License*: unknown *Contributors*: -

Image:Usina Hidreletrica de Sobradinho-BA.jpg *Source*: http://bibliocm.bibliolabs.com/mwAnon/index.php?title=File:Usina_Hidreletrica_de_Sobradinho-BA.jpg *License*: unknown *Contributors*: -

Image:Igrejinha de Porto Seguro.jpg *Source*: http://bibliocm.bibliolabs.com/mwAnon/index.php?title=File:Igrejinha_de_Porto_Seguro.jpg *License*: unknown *Contributors*: -

Image:Vale do Pati.jpg *Source*: http://bibliocm.bibliolabs.com/mwAnon/index.php?title=File:Vale_do_Pati.jpg *License*: unknown *Contributors*: -

Image:Bloco da Capoeira, Circuito Campo Grande 2008.jpg *Source*: http://bibliocm.bibliolabs.com/mwAnon/index.php?title=File:Bloco_da_Capoeira,_Circuito_Campo_Grande_2008.jpg *License*: unknown *Contributors*: -

Image:Salvador-CCBY-2.jpg *Source*: http://bibliocm.bibliolabs.com/mwAnon/index.php?title=File:Salvador-CCBY-2.jpg *License*: Creative Commons Attribution 2.0 *Contributors*: joquerollo

Image:Linha Verde2.jpg *Source*: http://bibliocm.bibliolabs.com/mwAnon/index.php?title=File:Linha_Verde2.jpg *License*: unknown *Contributors*: -

Image:Bahia transportes.png *Source*: http://bibliocm.bibliolabs.com/mwAnon/index.php?title=File:Bahia_transportes.png *License*: unknown *Contributors*: -

Image:UnebVI.jpg *Source*: http://bibliocm.bibliolabs.com/mwAnon/index.php?title=File:UnebVI.jpg *License*: unknown *Contributors*: -

File:Samba Parade - Rio's Carnival 2008.jpg *Source*: http://bibliocm.bibliolabs.com/mwAnon/index.php?title=File:Samba_Parade_-_Rio's_Carnival_2008.jpg *License*: unknown *Contributors*: -

File:Speaker Icon.svg *Source*: http://bibliocm.bibliolabs.com/mwAnon/index.php?title=File:Speaker_Icon.svg *License*: unknown *Contributors*: -

File:Batuque.jpg *Source*: http://bibliocm.bibliolabs.com/mwAnon/index.php?title=File:Batuque.jpg *License*: unknown *Contributors*: -

File:Zeca Pagodinho.jpg *Source*: http://bibliocm.bibliolabs.com/mwAnon/index.php?title=File:Zeca_Pagodinho.jpg *License*: unknown *Contributors*: -

Image:Rugendasroda.jpg *Source*: http://bibliocm.bibliolabs.com/mwAnon/index.php?title=File:Rugendasroda.jpg *License*: unknown *Contributors*: -

Image:Capoeira-three-berimbau-one-pandeiro.jpg *Source*: http://bibliocm.bibliolabs.com/mwAnon/index.php?title=File:Capoeira-three-berimbau-one-pandeiro.jpg *License*: unknown *Contributors*: -

Image:Capoeira Dance.jpg *Source*: http://bibliocm.bibliolabs.com/mwAnon/index.php?title=File:Capoeira_Dance.jpg *License*: unknown *Contributors*: -

Image:Auangole.gif *Source*: http://bibliocm.bibliolabs.com/mwAnon/index.php?title=File:Auangole.gif *License*: unknown *Contributors*: -

File:Montagem Salvador.jpg *Source*: http://bibliocm.bibliolabs.com/mwAnon/index.php?title=File:Montagem_Salvador.jpg *License*: unknown *Contributors*: -

File:Brazil location map.svg *Source*: http://bibliocm.bibliolabs.com/mwAnon/index.php?title=File:Brazil_location_map.svg *License*: unknown *Contributors*: -

File:Red pog.svg *Source*: http://bibliocm.bibliolabs.com/mwAnon/index.php?title=File:Red_pog.svg *License*: unknown *Contributors*: -

File:Campo Grande ssa.jpg *Source*: http://bibliocm.bibliolabs.com/mwAnon/index.php?title=File:Campo_Grande_ssa.jpg *License*: unknown *Contributors*: -

File:Lindo Sol em Plataforma.jpg *Source*: http://bibliocm.bibliolabs.com/mwAnon/index.php?title=File:Lindo_Sol_em_Plataforma.jpg *License*: unknown *Contributors*: -

File:Salvador-CCBY-4.jpg *Source*: http://bibliocm.bibliolabs.com/mwAnon/index.php?title=File:Salvador-CCBY-4.jpg *License*: unknown *Contributors*: -

File:Salvador-CCBY-5.jpg *Source*: http://bibliocm.bibliolabs.com/mwAnon/index.php?title=File:Salvador-CCBY-5.jpg *License*: unknown *Contributors*: -

File:Salvador-CCBY-2.jpg *Source*: http://bibliocm.bibliolabs.com/mwAnon/index.php?title=File:Salvador-CCBY-2.jpg *License*: Creative Commons Attribution 2.0 *Contributors*: joquerollo

File:20604PelourinhoBahiaBrazil.jpg *Source*: http://bibliocm.bibliolabs.com/mwAnon/index.php?title=File:20604PelourinhoBahiaBrazil.jpg *License*: unknown *Contributors*: -

File:Forte s diogo vista aerea salvador.jpg *Source*: http://bibliocm.bibliolabs.com/mwAnon/index.php?title=File:Forte_s_diogo_vista_aerea_salvador.jpg *License*: unknown *Contributors*: -

File:Anchieta Pelourinho Cyark.jpg *Source*: http://bibliocm.bibliolabs.com/mwAnon/index.php?title=File:Anchieta_Pelourinho_Cyark.jpg *License*: unknown *Contributors*: -

File:IURD Salvador - A Casa da Moeda.jpg *Source*: http://bibliocm.bibliolabs.com/mwAnon/index.php?title=File:IURD_Salvador_-_A_Casa_da_Moeda.jpg *License*: unknown *Contributors*: -

File:500x375 traditional bahia street kitchen salvador da bahia brasil.jpg *Source*: http://bibliocm.bibliolabs.com/mwAnon/index.php?title=File:500x375_traditional_bahia_street_kitchen_salvador_da_bahia_brasil.jpg *License*: unknown *Contributors*: -

File:Bloco da Capoeira, Circuito Campo Grande 2008.jpg *Source*: http://bibliocm.bibliolabs.com/mwAnon/index.php?title=File:Bloco_da_Capoeira,_Circuito_Campo_Grande_2008.jpg *License*: unknown *Contributors*: -

File:View over Harbour Area from Hotel Arthemis - Salvador - Brazil.jpg *Source*: http://bibliocm.bibliolabs.com/mwAnon/index.php?title=File:View_over_Harbour_Area_from_Hotel_Arthemis_-_Salvador_-_Brazil.jpg *License*: unknown *Contributors*: -

File:Carniaval Salvador Bahia Brazil 1997.jpg *Source*: http://bibliocm.bibliolabs.com/mwAnon/index.php?title=File:Carniaval_Salvador_Bahia_Brazil_1997.jpg *License*: unknown *Contributors*: -

File:Anfiteatro do Parque da Cidade de Salvador 2.jpg *Source*: http://bibliocm.bibliolabs.com/mwAnon/index.php?title=File:Anfiteatro_do_Parque_da_Cidade_de_Salvador_2.jpg *License*: unknown *Contributors*: -

File:Linha Verde2.jpg *Source*: http://bibliocm.bibliolabs.com/mwAnon/index.php?title=File:Linha_Verde2.jpg *License*: unknown *Contributors*: -

File:2º Distrito Naval Salvador.jpeg *Source*: http://bibliocm.bibliolabs.com/mwAnon/index.php?title=File:2º_Distrito_Naval_Salvador.jpeg *License*: unknown *Contributors*: -

Image Sources, Licenses and Contributors

File:Bahia.JPG *Source*: http://bibliocm.bibliolabs.com/mwAnon/index.php?title=File:Bahia.JPG *License*: Public Domain *Contributors*: Bukk, Hämbörger, Leonardorejorge, Luke Chiconi, Priwo, Raquelalina, Wknight94, 3 anonymous edits

File:Skate no Jardim dos Namorados.jpg *Source*: http://bibliocm.bibliolabs.com/mwAnon/index.php?title=File:Skate_no_Jardim_dos_Namorados.jpg *License*: unknown *Contributors*: -

File:Flag of Namibia.svg *Source*: http://bibliocm.bibliolabs.com/mwAnon/index.php?title=File:Flag_of_Namibia.svg *License*: unknown *Contributors*: -

File:Flag of Vanuatu.svg *Source*: http://bibliocm.bibliolabs.com/mwAnon/index.php?title=File:Flag_of_Vanuatu.svg *License*: unknown *Contributors*: -

File:Flag of Guatemala.svg *Source*: http://bibliocm.bibliolabs.com/mwAnon/index.php?title=File:Flag_of_Guatemala.svg *License*: unknown *Contributors*: -

File:Victoria's Secret models visit Guantanamo, December 2007.jpg *Source*: http://bibliocm.bibliolabs.com/mwAnon/index.php?title=File:Victoria's_Secret_models_visit_Guantanamo._December_2007.jpg *License*: unknown *Contributors*: -

File:Flag of the United States.svg *Source*: http://bibliocm.bibliolabs.com/mwAnon/index.php?title=File:Flag_of_the_United_States.svg *License*: unknown *Contributors*: -

File:Flag of Portugal.svg *Source*: http://bibliocm.bibliolabs.com/mwAnon/index.php?title=File:Flag_of_Portugal.svg *License*: unknown *Contributors*: -

File:Flag of Spain.svg *Source*: http://bibliocm.bibliolabs.com/mwAnon/index.php?title=File:Flag_of_Spain.svg *License*: unknown *Contributors*: -

File:Flag of Italy.svg *Source*: http://bibliocm.bibliolabs.com/mwAnon/index.php?title=File:Flag_of_Italy.svg *License*: unknown *Contributors*: -

File:Flag of the People's Republic of China.svg *Source*: http://bibliocm.bibliolabs.com/mwAnon/index.php?title=File:Flag_of_the_People's_Republic_of_China.svg *License*: unknown *Contributors*: -

Image:Salvador 0 Barra.png *Source*: http://bibliocm.bibliolabs.com/mwAnon/index.php?title=File:Salvador_0_Barra.png *License*: unknown *Contributors*: -

File:Salvador decada 70 porto da barra desfile maritimo.jpg *Source*: http://bibliocm.bibliolabs.com/mwAnon/index.php?title=File:Salvador_decada_70_porto_da_barra_desfile_maritimo.jpg *License*: unknown *Contributors*: -

File:Salvador decada 70 porto da barra.jpg *Source*: http://bibliocm.bibliolabs.com/mwAnon/index.php?title=File:Salvador_decada_70_porto_da_barra.jpg *License*: unknown *Contributors*: -

File:SalvadorBarraFortress-CCBY.jpg *Source*: http://bibliocm.bibliolabs.com/mwAnon/index.php?title=File:SalvadorBarraFortress-CCBY.jpg *License*: unknown *Contributors*: -

File:Praia do Porto da Barra 1.jpg *Source*: http://bibliocm.bibliolabs.com/mwAnon/index.php?title=File:Praia_do_Porto_da_Barra_1.jpg *License*: unknown *Contributors*: -

Image:Salvador 2 Brotas.png *Source*: http://bibliocm.bibliolabs.com/mwAnon/index.php?title=File:Salvador_2_Brotas.png *License*: unknown *Contributors*: -

File:Salvador 1 detalhe Porto Centro Histórico.png *Source*: http://bibliocm.bibliolabs.com/mwAnon/index.php?title=File:Salvador_1_detalhe_Porto_Centro_Histórico.png *License*: unknown *Contributors*: -

File:Salvador-CamaraVereadores.jpg *Source*: http://bibliocm.bibliolabs.com/mwAnon/index.php?title=File:Salvador-CamaraVereadores.jpg *License*: unknown *Contributors*: -

File:Street Scene - Salvador - Brazil 02.jpg *Source*: http://bibliocm.bibliolabs.com/mwAnon/index.php?title=File:Street_Scene_-_Salvador_-_Brazil_02.jpg *License*: unknown *Contributors*: -

Image:Salvador 0 Ondina.png *Source*: http://bibliocm.bibliolabs.com/mwAnon/index.php?title=File:Salvador_0_Ondina.png *License*: unknown *Contributors*: -

File:Pituba de noite.jpg *Source*: http://bibliocm.bibliolabs.com/mwAnon/index.php?title=File:Pituba_de_noite.jpg *License*: unknown *Contributors*: -

Image:Salvador Vitória mapa.png *Source*: http://bibliocm.bibliolabs.com/mwAnon/index.php?title=File:Salvador_Vitória_mapa.png *License*: unknown *Contributors*: -

Image:StFranciscoChurch1-CCBY.jpg *Source*: http://bibliocm.bibliolabs.com/mwAnon/index.php?title=File:StFranciscoChurch1-CCBY.jpg *License*: unknown *Contributors*: -

Image:StFranciscoChurch3-CCBY.jpg *Source*: http://bibliocm.bibliolabs.com/mwAnon/index.php?title=File:StFranciscoChurch3-CCBY.jpg *License*: unknown *Contributors*: -

Image:NSBonfim-Salvador1-CCBYSA.jpg *Source*: http://bibliocm.bibliolabs.com/mwAnon/index.php?title=File:NSBonfim-Salvador1-CCBYSA.jpg *License*: unknown *Contributors*: -

File:Avenida 7 de Setembro (Salvador - Bahia).png *Source*: http://bibliocm.bibliolabs.com/mwAnon/index.php?title=File:Avenida_7_de_Setembro_(Salvador_-_Bahia).png *License*: unknown *Contributors*: -

File:Avenida Sete de Setembro.jpg *Source*: http://bibliocm.bibliolabs.com/mwAnon/index.php?title=File:Avenida_Sete_de_Setembro.jpg *License*: unknown *Contributors*: -

file: Grande Sertao Veredas 1.jpg *Source*: http://bibliocm.bibliolabs.com/mwAnon/index.php?title=File:Grande_Sertao_Veredas_1.jpg *License*: unknown *Contributors*: -

Image:Grande Sertao Veredas 2.jpg *Source*: http://bibliocm.bibliolabs.com/mwAnon/index.php?title=File:Grande_Sertao_Veredas_2.jpg *License*: unknown *Contributors*: -

Image:Grande Sertao Veredas 4.jpg *Source*: http://bibliocm.bibliolabs.com/mwAnon/index.php?title=File:Grande_Sertao_Veredas_4.jpg *License*: unknown *Contributors*: -

file: Chapada diamantina.jpg *Source*: http://bibliocm.bibliolabs.com/mwAnon/index.php?title=File:Chapada_diamantina.jpg *License*: unknown *Contributors*: -

Image:chapada diamantina flora.jpg *Source*: http://bibliocm.bibliolabs.com/mwAnon/index.php?title=File:Chapada_diamantina_flora.jpg *License*: unknown *Contributors*: -

File:FarolMorroSaoPaulo.jpg *Source*: http://bibliocm.bibliolabs.com/mwAnon/index.php?title=File:FarolMorroSaoPaulo.jpg *License*: unknown *Contributors*: -

Image:Elevador bahia.jpg *Source*: http://bibliocm.bibliolabs.com/mwAnon/index.php?title=File:Elevador_bahia.jpg *License*: unknown *Contributors*: -

Image:Salvador e Baía de Todos os Santos.jpg *Source*: http://bibliocm.bibliolabs.com/mwAnon/index.php?title=File:Salvador_e_Baía_de_Todos_os_Santos.jpg *License*: unknown *Contributors*: -

Image:ECV Campeão Baiano 1908.jpg *Source*: http://bibliocm.bibliolabs.com/mwAnon/index.php?title=File:ECV_Campeão_Baiano_1908.jpg *License*: unknown *Contributors*: -

File:Flag of Serbia.svg *Source*: http://bibliocm.bibliolabs.com/mwAnon/index.php?title=File:Flag_of_Serbia.svg *License*: unknown *Contributors*: -

File:Flag of Ecuador.svg *Source*: http://bibliocm.bibliolabs.com/mwAnon/index.php?title=File:Flag_of_Ecuador.svg *License*: unknown *Contributors*: -

Image Sources, Licenses and Contributors

File:Flag of France.svg *Source*: http://bibliocm.bibliolabs.com/mwAnon/index.php?title=File:Flag_of_France.svg *License*: unknown *Contributors*: -

File:Flag of Brazil (1968-1992).svg *Source*: http://bibliocm.bibliolabs.com/mwAnon/index.php?title=File:Flag_of_Brazil_(1968-1992).svg *License*: unknown *Contributors*: -

File:Flag of Peru.svg *Source*: http://bibliocm.bibliolabs.com/mwAnon/index.php?title=File:Flag_of_Peru.svg *License*: unknown *Contributors*: -

File:Flag of Sweden.svg *Source*: http://bibliocm.bibliolabs.com/mwAnon/index.php?title=File:Flag_of_Sweden.svg *License*: unknown *Contributors*: -

File:Flag of Mexico.svg *Source*: http://bibliocm.bibliolabs.com/mwAnon/index.php?title=File:Flag_of_Mexico.svg *License*: unknown *Contributors*: -

File:2116RP037.jpg *Source*: http://bibliocm.bibliolabs.com/mwAnon/index.php?title=File:2116RP037.jpg *License*: unknown *Contributors*: -

Image:Fonte Nova2.jpg *Source*: http://bibliocm.bibliolabs.com/mwAnon/index.php?title=File:Fonte_Nova2.jpg *License*: unknown *Contributors*: -

Image:Jogo barradao.jpg *Source*: http://bibliocm.bibliolabs.com/mwAnon/index.php?title=File:Jogo_barradao.jpg *License*: unknown *Contributors*: -

File:08814 w.JPG *Source*: http://bibliocm.bibliolabs.com/mwAnon/index.php?title=File:08814_w.JPG *License*: Public Domain *Contributors*: Dantadd, Luan, Michel Meunier, Raphael.lorenzeto, 1 anonymous edits

File:Bahia Municip PortoSeguro.svg *Source*: http://bibliocm.bibliolabs.com/mwAnon/index.php?title=File:Bahia_Municip_PortoSeguro.svg *License*: unknown *Contributors*: -

File:Br-ba-fs.jpg *Source*: http://bibliocm.bibliolabs.com/mwAnon/index.php?title=File:Br-ba-fs.jpg *License*: unknown *Contributors*: -

File:Brasao feira.jpg *Source*: http://bibliocm.bibliolabs.com/mwAnon/index.php?title=File:Brasao_feira.jpg *License*: unknown *Contributors*: -

File:VDC parcial.jpg *Source*: http://bibliocm.bibliolabs.com/mwAnon/index.php?title=File:VDC_parcial.jpg *License*: unknown *Contributors*: -

File:Ilheus, Bahia 1.jpg *Source*: http://bibliocm.bibliolabs.com/mwAnon/index.php?title=File:Ilheus,_Bahia_1.jpg *License*: unknown *Contributors*: -

File:Bahia Municip Ilheus.svg *Source*: http://bibliocm.bibliolabs.com/mwAnon/index.php?title=File:Bahia_Municip_Ilheus.svg *License*: unknown *Contributors*: -

image:Bahia Municip Itabuna.svg *Source*: http://bibliocm.bibliolabs.com/mwAnon/index.php?title=File:Bahia_Municip_Itabuna.svg *License*: unknown *Contributors*: -

File:ITABUNA_SKYLINE.jpg *Source*: http://bibliocm.bibliolabs.com/mwAnon/index.php?title=File:ITABUNA_SKYLINE.jpg *License*: unknown *Contributors*: -

Image:Bahia Municip Cachoeira.svg *Source*: http://bibliocm.bibliolabs.com/mwAnon/index.php?title=File:Bahia_Municip_Cachoeira.svg *License*: unknown *Contributors*: -

File:Salvador 2 detalhe Aeroporto.png *Source*: http://bibliocm.bibliolabs.com/mwAnon/index.php?title=File:Salvador_2_detalhe_Aeroporto.png *License*: unknown *Contributors*: -

File:SalvadorDaBahiaMetroLapa.jpg *Source*: http://bibliocm.bibliolabs.com/mwAnon/index.php?title=File:SalvadorDaBahiaMetroLapa.jpg *License*: unknown *Contributors*: -

CPSIA information can be obtained at www.ICGtesting.com
Printed in the USA
BVOW02s1652301014

373021BV00005B/40/P

9 781249 224570